Eric Falque and Sarah-J

Addressing Customer Paradoxes...

in the Digital World

PEARSON

Addressing Customer Paradoxes...

Layout: FAB Orléans

ISBN: 978-2-7440-6488-3

Contents

UNDERSTAND your customers' psychology
and help them deal with paradoxes

TRANSACT efficiently

EXPERIENCE differently in a digital world

RELATE in a social environment

PREPARE your organisation for tomorrow's challenges

Foreword

Customer Management is about providing a customised experience to selected customers at the most efficient cost.

But the new digital world is dramatically transforming the way customers will transact, relate and experience along with the business models associated with these changes.

We gathered experts from BearingPoint, academics and sociologists and discovered what we called "the Digital Paradoxes": what shapes customer behaviours in the digital space is very often ubiquitous (i.e. "I want to pay in one click and/but I want maximum security on my payments").

We strongly believe that understanding and dealing effectively with those paradoxes will make the difference between successful companies and the others in the near future. But this is just the first step: how do companies need to adapt their organisation, processes and required competences to become more reactive across departments and channels is the second key challenge.

This collective work, illustrated with numerous examples, should help you build your opinion on the future of Customer Management in a Digital World.

You can either read it from the beginning to the end, or simply dip into the chapters that interest you. In order to guide you, we have divided the book into five parts: Understand, Transact, Experience, Relate and Prepare.

Understand presents the paradoxes described above. *Transact* analyses the existing customer channels and suggests improvements to match, starting now, the points of contact to the new customer behaviour. *Experience* describes some new ways to interact with the customers. *Relate* emphasises the impact of social networking on how a company interacts with its customers, and provides a lot of details on how to leverage those social interactions through technology. Finally, *Prepare* suggests recommendations to adapt organisations to the digital age.

This book is a practical guide. It has been written by consultants who help large companies transform themselves on a day-to-day basis. Thus, it provides real life examples, but also keys to enter this emerging world. We are pleased to share with you our thoughts and experience, and hope you will enjoy reading about our findings.

Eric FALQUE

Introduction

Ten years of the digital consumer

OUR LIFE BEHIND THE SCREENS: A SENSE OF PARADOX.

The digital world, incorporating the internet, PCs and mobile phones, is barely 20 years old. Yet 28.7% of the world's population already use the internet – some 2 billion people.[1] BearingPoint estimates that up to 1.7 billion consumers have shopped online.[2] The proportion of all adults ordering goods and services online are 45% in France,[3] 56% in Germany, 62% in the UK and even more in the US.[4] The digital consumer is well and truly with us.

Though Amazon launched online in 1995 and eBay followed in 1996, these business models were originally considered to be novelties. Accordingly the *mass market* of digital consumers can only really be considered to have existed for about 10 years. It is important not to overstate the role of "pure" digital commerce however. As a percentage of total retail sales, internet sales, as recorded in economic statistics, still account for under 10% by value. But the internet is frequently involved in physical sales as well. Indeed, physical and virtual channels are increasingly intertwined, with product search and evaluation undertaken in one channel and purchase completed in another. It is not unusual to surf a virtual store for prices and reviews while simultaneously shopping in a real store with the intention of picking up goods immediately.

Ten years is not long in economic history, and it is only just enough time to discern meaningful insights and comment on future challenges. We are still in a period of experimentation and rapid developments, but the landscape contours can be seen. One must be careful, however, not to make sweeping inferences based on phenomena that may turn out to be passing fads. A case in point is Second Life. Genuinely innovative it may have been, but its currently dwindling user base implies that most people choose to stick to their first life.

While we will discuss digital *consumers* later, we need to start by looking at digital *users*. The extent to which people use digital media such as the internet, mobile phones or even digital TV varies according to their location and their demographics. Though men are more likely to use the internet than women, the most striking aspect of the digital landscape is the massive intergenerational disparity, which we turn to next.

Through the digital generations

There has never been such a stark difference between the generations, as shown in Figure I.1 based on the most recent statistics.[5]

The 10 years of mass internet use is a short time compared with people's lifetimes. It is not surprising that it matters whereabouts in a person's life that the mass internet revolution started. This is because people are typically less able to take on innovations or changes of any sort as they get older.[6] The *digital generation* has grown up with the internet and mobile phones; they know no different. The next generation are *digital transitioners* who did not grow up with the internet but have adapted pretty well. Finally there are the *digital toe-dippers* for whom the internet came late in their lives. The age boundaries are not sharp but the main characteristics of these three cohorts is shown in Figure I.2.

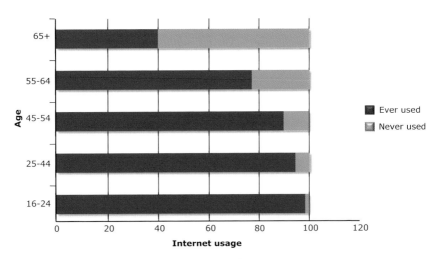

Figure I.1 Internet usage by age group, 2010

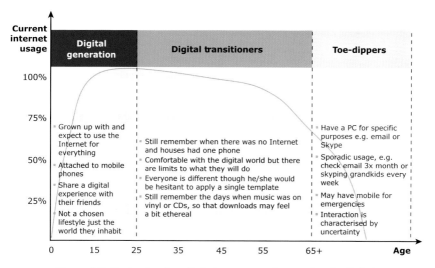

Figure I.2 Understanding digital customers (source BearingPoint)

Five unsolved paradoxes

Dealing with digital consumers is a lot more complicated than checking their age! BearingPoint has been through a process engaging its consultants across Europe and partners in the USA to take a hard look at the strategic issues around customer management in the digital space. Oddly, as the discussions went on, for every so called trend observed there seemed to be a counter-example. And so the idea emerged that there are some key "paradoxes" to the way in which digital consumers should be handled. The five paradoxes are illustrated in Figure I.3.

The first paradox is physical versus digital. The trend towards virtualisation started with the substitution of real products and services by digital ones. Then came the integration of physical and digital. Now we are entering a new phase in which exciting combinations of the real world and digital technology are being brought together in augmented reality applications. For example, software developer Zungara has developed applications to help people try on fashion items in virtual space and send pictures to their friends for approval. Because people – and companies – often want aspects of both the physical and the digital worlds, it is difficult to know which application will take off.

The second paradox is form versus function. Different types of website assume different types of user. A "form" website offers its audience an engaging experience, whereas a functional website prioritises quick and easy transactions. Sites like ladygaga.com emphasise form whereas most online banking websites are

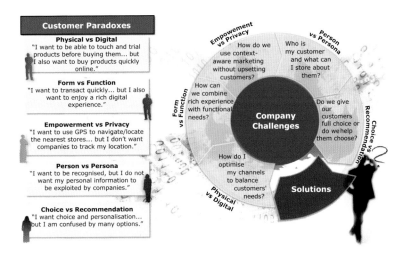

Figure I.3 Five unsolved paradoxes

purely functional. Ideally, websites and mobile applications should be sensitive to customers' state of mind. If you are at a station using a smartphone to buy a train ticket you probably don't want to be forced to watch a video about trains. How can you ensure that your website hits the mark?

The third paradox is the tension between privacy and the useful applications that can be offered if the requirement for privacy is relaxed; we call this opposite pole "empowerment". To take some examples, many consumers welcomed Google Street View, but not all. Residents of the English village of Broughton formed a human chain in 2009 to prevent Google from taking pictures of their homes amid fears that the images could be used by burglars.[7] Location-based apps on mobile phones were used by over half the respondents to a 2010 Microsoft survey[8] and 94% of respondents considered these services to be valuable. But 52% expressed strong concern about sharing their location with other people or organisations. This concern is higher for sharing location with organisations as opposed to other people, though this varies by country. US consumers are more concerned (56%) whereas Japanese consumers are less concerned (39%).

The fourth paradox is about the level of disclosure customers make; we have called this "person versus persona". When someone files their income tax with the Inland Revenue they do so as a person. All their real details are required – at least in theory! By contrast, a player on Second Life can act through an entirely imaginary persona. Between these extremes are a range of options about how much of the real person is revealed. As a business, how much should you force customers to disclose about themselves? There might be a gap between the information you want and the information that customers are comfortable in disclosing.

The fifth paradox is choice versus recommendation. Too much choice is bewildering, but some people can be wary of receiving recommendations. Companies are faced with challenges about how to make choice manageable. Which is better, to artificially restrict choice or to offer computer-based recommendations?

These paradoxes apply to both customers and companies. Customers may want incompatible goals. For example, they may want only to receive relevant information from advertisers, but for the purposes of privacy may simultaneously require that no information about their personal interests and past purchases be collated to provide the information base for that targeting. Companies have to make choices about their customer management strategies, and such choices risk alienating some customers while enticing others. Businesses have to consciously recognise these paradoxes and decide where they stand. Some businesses will challenge consumers' comfort zones, stretching the paradoxes. Others will learn from the mistakes of other businesses and stick with what is known to work.

Human psychology re-expressed in the digital age

A key contributing factor is the extent to which technology has opened up new possibilities, but that these new possibilities are sometimes at odds with current sensibilities. The debates around the behavioural targeting software Webwise, developed by Phorm, illustrate this paradox. Webwise looks deep inside users' internet traffic, scrutinises their browsing habits and uses this data to enable highly targeted advertising. Originally promoted to ISPs, Phorm's software tended to be covert – with the result that it was branded spyware. In the face of questions about both the legality and the morality of Phorm's approach, recent versions of the software require users to "opt in". It seems that Phorm originally took a step too far.

The Phorm story is not an aberration. Technology has the capacity to store, integrate and process behavioural data, using data mining of weak information signals to provide valuable information about individuals. The problem is, these developments are starting to be implemented without fully informed consent. No one knows what consumers' reactions will be, and whether legislators will take a stand. One way around the problem of how to interpret and respond to a digital revolution that is barely 10 years old, is to recognise that human psychology remains largely unchanged. People are sociable, they seek friendship, they care about trust, they interact with the world both cognitively and emotionally. These truths remain, but must be re-expressed in the digital age.

Emotionally intelligent digital interactions?

In 2010 the Leiden Institute of Advanced Computer Science in The Netherlands organised an international conference on Human-Robot Personal Relationships.[9] Billed as an opportunity to discuss studies of personal relationships with artificial partners, the ideas sound at first like science fiction. Until one realises that through telemedicine, electronic devices are already substituting for care workers in healthcare. If such applications are designed to be more approachable and friendly, the chances are they will be used more effectively.

Since the early days, psychologists have looked at people's digital interactions. Stanford University professor Byron Reeves observed that "humans are not evolved to respond to 20th century technology". Instead, in his book *The Media Equation*, he argues that people treat computers, television and new media like real people and places. How can that be? Reeves argues that, when presented with human-like cues, individuals are swayed by the human characteristics and do not process the fact that the machine is not human. And if people treat digital media like people, they'll look for some of the same characteristics.

Which brings us on to the idea of emotional intelligence. Emotional intelligence (EI) is the name given to the traits and skills that make some people excel at reading and influencing other people's emotions. Studies have found that EI is correlated with career success, and psychometric tests have even been developed to measure EI. Like much in the social sciences, there is plenty of debate about what this all means.

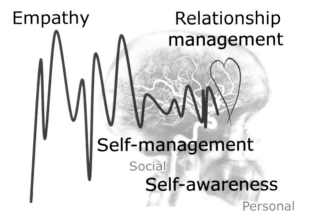

Figure I.4 Emotional intelligence

Daniel Goleman, who popularised the concept, may have overstated the case, but most experts agree that EI ingredients have some validity.[10]

So can we talk about digital interaction strategies having emotional intelligence? They can certainly be designed to. Thanks to cookies, a website can address you by your first name, remember where you left off, and respect your preferences. It may only be a digital screen saying "welcome back, Paul" but Paul will subconsciously feel stroked; even if Paul knows full well it's driven by a computer he can't help being influenced. This is just the start. Just as people pick up on subliminal clues to other people's psychological state – such as micro facial expressions – there are numerous clues available to digital touch points to decode the state of the humans they interact with. Emotionally intelligent websites can monitor the delays before key strokes and adjust to your perceived mood; voice processing can spot signs of anxiety by analysing the frequency spectrum of your voice.

An emotionally intelligent digital interaction strategy would act appropriately in social situations. The German sociologist Max Weber recognised that social norms and rules guard against the misuse of power. The growth of campaign groups around internet privacy is an indication that these norms are starting to be contested.

The theme of emotional intelligence will be revisited throughout this book. But the main focus is on the five paradoxes introduced earlier. These are the dimensions in which customers and companies are faced with interdependent choices. The choices will also depend on age cohort, a topic that will be picked up again in the Conclusions section at the end of this book.

Follow us on this journey trough this series of articles and standpoints that the BearingPoint teams have gathered for you. The first part, Understand, focuses on customers psychology and how they handle paradoxes in their digital life. The second part, Transact, efficiently includes a broad range of convictions on how to optimise the purchase funnel using various means. The third part, Experience, provides an original approach of the customer management in the digital world, while the part entitled Relate exposes various assets of an extended ecosystem. The last part, Prepare your organisation, suggests alternatives for tomorrow's challenges.

Notes

1. http://www.internetworldstats.com/stats.htm
2. Extrapolated from http://id.nielsen.com/news/documents/GlobalOnlineShoppingReportFeb08.pdf
3. http://www.internetretailing.net/2010/11/uk-leads-europe-in-internet-shopping/
4. http://www.statistics.gov.uk/pdfdir/iahi0810.pdf
5. http://www.statistics.gov.uk/pdfdir/iahi0810.pdf
6. Rogers, E. (2003). *Diffusion of Innovations*, Fifth Edition. Free Press.
7. http://www.telegraph.co.uk/technology/google/5095241/Google-Street-View-Residents-block-street-to-prevent-filming-over-crime-fears.html
8. http://www.microsoft.com/privacy/dpd/
9. http://hrpr.liacs.nl/
10. List based on Goleman, D. (1995). *Emotional Intelligence: Why It Can Matter More Than IQ*. London: Bloomsbury.

UNDERSTAND your customers' psychology and help them deal with paradoxes

Paradox 1

Physical versus digital

SO REAL, YOU COULD ALMOST DOWNLOAD IT.

Virtualisation

Prompted by growing use of computers, commentators in the 1970s such as Alvin Toffler predicted a future post-industrial world increasingly dominated by information – so much so that citizens would be disorientated by information overload. While some of these predictions have been borne out, the central message of a "future shock" was unduly pessimistic. Instead of being swamped, consumers have generally embraced information technologies and the substitution of physical artefacts by virtual ones. This is despite the adage that people are resistant to change. While we all complain about the number of emails we receive and the problems of spam, few of us would willingly return to the time when using the postal service was the only option (see Figure 1.1).

Where the futurologists were right was in their predictions of the pace and extent of change. Almost no aspect of daily life is now immune from the possibilities opened up by PCs and smartphones. Virtualisation – substituting or augmenting physical artefacts with virtual ones – presents opportunities for innovation on an unprecedented scale. Greater degrees of product personalisation are made possible and products can be delivered directly on to portable electronic devices (e.g. books, maps, music). Established companies can suffer as product categories and traditional business models get wiped out.

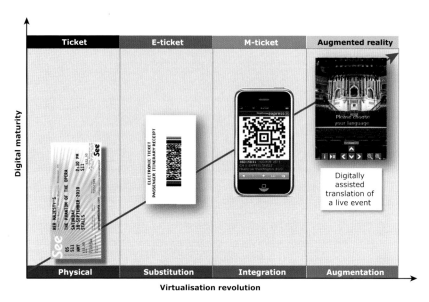

Figure 1.1 Substitution, integration and augmentation (source BearingPoint)

The changing accommodation between real and virtual components is taking place in products themselves, the purchasing process and customer support (see Figure 1.2).

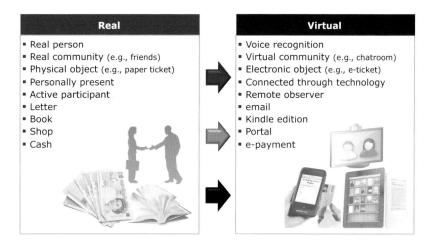

Figure 1.2 Real versus virtual (source BearingPoint)

Phase I: Substitution

The first phase of the virtualisation revolution was the *direct substitution* of traditional products and associated sales processes by virtual equivalents, driven predominantly by cost reduction. Early online retailing concentrated on products that consumers were familiar with such as books, music, airline tickets and computer hardware and software. In some cases this virtualisation predated the internet; in insurance, for example, telesales was already well established as an alternative to traditional car insurance broking by the time that the internet started to be used. While there is still scope for direct substitution, leading to more and more goods going digital, the easy areas have been done, and the ones that are left are becoming more tenuous. There is genuine doubt over how far the trend towards virtualisation will go. A case in point is prescription glasses. It might be assumed that a health-related product that traditionally involves trained opticians at the point of sale would be an unlikely candidate for an online sales channel. But online opticians do indeed exist, though whether they will ever seriously dent the profits of high street chains is debatable.

A recent driver for substitution has been environmental concern. The UK media regulator Ofcom sponsored research concluding that communication systems have significant potential to provide positive environmental benefits, especially with respect to reducing the emissions that result from travel.[1]

Some substitutions turn out to be unpopular with consumers – for example replacing bank branches with call centres. Others are more difficult to judge, such as the pros and cons of a printed manual as opposed to a web link. The UK consumer organisation, Which?, recently asked its members, "Do you miss the printed instruction booklet?". Most, but not all, were still in favour of manuals for complex, high-value products. Cost reductions or even environmental benefits may hold little attraction for consumers.

To make some substitutions occur, manufacturers sometimes have to engineer digital products to incorporate the reassuring characteristics of the old. The electronic click of a digital camera replicates the sound of an old mechanical shutter, but reproducing this exact sound has no functional purpose.

Part of the paradox is that consumers seek contradictory goals. Research has shown that there are many different attributes that people consider when deciding which channel to use. These attributes include shopping enjoyment; shopping speed; having a large selection; the best price; seeing, touching and handling; personal service; speedy delivery; and "no hassle exchange". The weighting of these attributes varies between types of product, and between individuals. For example, on a scale of 1 to 10, shopping for airline tickets rates 3.7 on the enjoyment scale whereas clothing rates 7.25 (and that's the average between males and females!).[2] Shopping is often a sociable experience.

Phase II: Integration

As the opportunities for further direct substitution reduce, a second phase of virtualisation is under way. This involves the *integration of real and virtual experiences* to create genuinely new forms of engagement. The role of digital technology in this phase goes well beyond merely replicating its physical counterpart. Whereas the first phase relied on PCs, this phase will build on the capabilities of mobile devices where their ability to relate to customers wherever they are on the go, and in real time, has no equivalent. Reader apps enable consumers to access product information and videos at retail using mobile barcodes (QR codes) or even just by photographing a product. The information is often generic but is starting to be integrated with pre-existing customer data and location. Electronic business cards that integrate with computer applications are an example of integration from the B2B world. The strategic consequence of this integration is the blurring of previously distinct parts of the buying process. Instead of a standardised linear process, customers

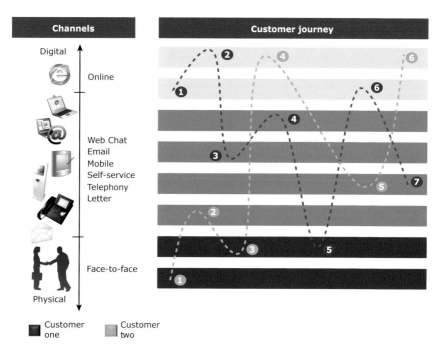

Figure 1.3 Two different customer journeys (source BearingPoint)

now enjoy physical and virtual interactions through a more individual "customer journey". As illustrated in Figure 1.3, which shows two different customers and their respective journeys, a multitude of channels and touch points are involved. In many markets it is now more important to differentiate the customer experience than differentiate products.

Customers expect a consistent and seamless experience across these multiple touch points, and expect to resume their journey where they left off: a form of "conversation" across different channels. Humans are brilliant at detecting inconsistencies – which is why inconsistencies are used in psychology experiments to study child development. For companies, inconsistencies erode a customer's ability to form a coherent understanding of brands and products. The trouble is, consistency can be difficult to achieve. One step is to synchronise customer contact history across channels. But many organisations depend on different legacy systems, so moving towards a cross-channel customer contact history requires significant investments and extensive organisational transformation. Unlike direct substitution, which was partly driven by the search for cost reductions, this phase may increase cost.

Phase III: Augmentation

The biggest challenge is in using digital technology to help sell products and services that are inherently physical in nature. Augmented reality applications are starting to emerge that allow physical experiences to be substituted by virtual experiences. For example, Zugara[3] has developed a software to enable people to try on virtual fashion items and, through social networking, to get their friends views on the look. At first this might seem like a poor substitute, but actually it's potentially much better. Fashion is, after all, about what other people think. What could be better than having a dozen second opinions before you buy? It is already common for friends to participate in shopping through video chats.

Technology isn't standing still

Augmented reality is part of a wider trend in technology. Gaming consoles were the first to use movement as an input and physical sensation as an output. These were followed by the iPhone and iPad, which took advantage of the extra dimension of physical movement. The co-founder of *Wired*, Kevin Kelly, has commented that interaction is still mainly limited to people's fingertips but that the iPad is changing this.[4] Looking ahead 20 years Kelly has claimed that there are six trends: screens on every surface; more modes of interaction including gestures, voice, cameras and movement; continuous tracking of everything we do; real-time streamed media; accessing material, not owning it; and copy protection.[5] Obviously these are personal views but they do accord with other forecasts that see the keyboard and screen losing their grip.

A generational perspective

Consumers are faced with the choice of what combination of physical and digital experience to go for, while companies have a bewildering choice of new configurations of real and digital and find it difficult to know where to invest. The digital generation seems more comfortable with the digital whereas the toe-dippers are less inclined to want to move away from the physical.

To recap, the main paradox here is that although we have a transition between broadly physical forms and broadly digital ones, customers still want aspects of the physical world and will make use of both physical and digital artefacts. So companies have to integrate the two and make judgements about what consumers will, or will not, accept in each channel. A conservative approach will not take full advantage of technology but a radical approach may fail to gain consumer acceptance.

Addressing the paradox

1. Map the roles of physical and digital channels in the customer journey space.
2. Research customer journeys in relation to your products and services. Understand how and why your customers use the respective channels.
3. Check that you are supporting the customer journey, integrating customer data and removing inconsistencies.
4. Identify substitution possibilities, ensuring that incentives are incorporated to promote the use of either physical or digital channels as appropriate.
5. Are there any tipping points in sight where the physical form becomes non-viable or marginalised?
6. Identify opportunities to integrate real and digital experiences.
7. Innovate. Think about opportunities to use new technologies such as augmented reality.

Notes

1. http://stakeholders.ofcom.org.uk/binaries/research/technology-research/environ.pdf
2. Levin, Levin & Heath, *Online Consumer Psychology*, p.406.
3. http://www.zugara.com/
4. http://techcrunch.com/2011/03/29/6-verbs/
5. http://techcrunch.com/2011/03/29/6-verbs/

Paradox 2

Form versus function

> I WANTED A TICKET AND ALL
> I GOT WAS A SHOPPING EXPERIENCE.

Audience or customer?

You want to find the details of a local car dealer in order to book a service. You visit the manufacturer's website and are greeted with a video of the latest model, which seems determined to load, together with pop-up advertising promotional deals. It takes 45 seconds to find the page you are looking for, but you are in a hurry and it's 45 seconds longer than you wanted. The video was irrelevant to you, in any case, as you are not looking for a new car.

A bad website? Not necessarily. If three years earlier you were looking for a new car, you might have been receptive to the video. The video, which is ingeniously tied into a TV campaign, has yielded stunning results.

The paradox here is about how companies see their website users. They can either be an "audience", looking for an engaging experience, or they can be customers, looking for a quick, efficient transaction. The matrix in Figure 2.1 shows how the experience on offer varies with the level of user involvement required. Low involvement and an emphasis on functionality are typically associated with e-commerce whereas high involvement and an emphasis on form is associated with brand awareness.

The trouble is, all users are different and even an individual user can be at different places in this matrix, depending on where they are in the purchasing

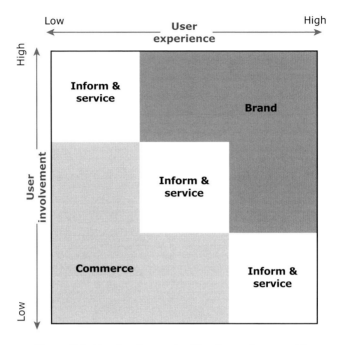

Figure 2.1 User involvement–offered experience matrix
(source BearingPoint)

cycle, and whether they are in a hurry or not. The key question is whether the interaction on offer matches the customer's state of mind at the time. If they match, there's no problem. If they do not, then either the customer gets frustrated or they do not get the reassurance they need and may fail to complete the transaction.

To help focus on the options it is worth thinking about the different roles that websites fulfil.

Websites and the attention economy

The first role is brand awareness, a role that can merge into that of a fan club. Used for categories as diverse as perfumes and pop stars, in their pure form these sites often encourage visitors to enjoy an experience and to share in a vision. Users don't care about the time it takes, so long as they're having a rich experience: a visit to ninaricci.com or ladygaga.com is not to be rushed. Indeed, the American theorist Michael Goldhaber has suggested that there is now an "attention economy".

Economies focus on what is scarce, and these days it's people's attention. Goldhaber asserts that "Money flows to attention, and much less well does attention flow to money", so if you hold people on your website you have accumulated a form of attention wealth.

Why would people spend their time (or devote their attention) to a website set up to offer a compelling brand identity to you or your product? What's in it for them? In a branch of sociology called cultural theory, it is often argued that these websites function to affirm the user's personal identity as well. Personal identity is not fixed but, instead, is "performed" through what people do. So as a customer, spending time on a website is, literally, investing time in constructing their identity.

Part of identity is being able to decode shared images and language. The more powerful such approaches are, the more prone they are to misrepresentation and misunderstanding. In February 2011 the UK's Advertising Standards Authority (ASA) banned an Yves Saint Laurent perfume advertisement because it included video said to simulate drug use. A longer version of the video was on the company's website, but at the time the ASA had no authority over digital media (though this has now changed). The case is fascinating because it rests on how different audiences would interpret edgy content. Was YSL's video being misunderstood, or was it being understood only too well?

As the capabilities of multimedia increase, companies will have the opportunity to present themselves not just in text and images but also with voice, tactile media etc., to elicit in users a sense of "presence" (being there and involvement in the mediated experience). The psychologists Nass and Sundar believe that when presented with physical cues that are related to fundamental human characteristics, individuals automatically respond socially.[1] Fortunately there are now more tools than ever to help design websites that mesh with users' psychology. Eye-tracking systems can be used in experiments to precisely measure how people scan and process websites. Personalisation is possible through the use of avatars and realistic animation sequences incorporating human facial expressions.

Trading platforms

At the other end of the spectrum, a website can function as a trading platform. Accumulated experience is that the more complicated and time consuming a website is, the less likely it is to be used. "One-click" ordering, retaining card details and simple verification procedures all make trading websites more effective. Unfortunately these innovations also make for greater security concerns. As yet, biometric techniques such as voice recognition, fingerprint recognition and iris scanning have failed to make it into consumer devices. Multi-platform verification of identities (for example, using a mobile text message to cross-check against a PC-based transaction) is increasingly popular.

Communities, information and support

Between the experiential and the transactional extremes there are several other roles for websites. One is to support the formation of communities – for example, reviews and user-generated content – broadly labelled Web 2.0. Studies have shown that dialogue generates commitment; giving customers an opportunity to comment on a company ties them in to a community, even if they are mildly critical. It is now normal for websites to either integrate with social media or to replicate aspects in house.

Another role of a website is as an information resource. It might be thought that the only consideration here is whether the information is easily accessible. However, the look and feel of a website still has to fit the audience. London's Metropolitan Police have a separate website aimed at young people with a more vibrant character than the more staid version for adults, as does the BBC news website.[2] CNN similarly provides a look and feel for its student news site that is different from its main site.[3]

Websites can also be the prime vehicle for the delivery of the customer experience – for example, Facebook and Google – or as the main way that customer service and support is delivered.

An experience surrounded by buttons

The diversity of roles for websites might at first imply that the different objectives cannot be met simultaneously. However many websites manage quite well. There is a de facto standard by which the central area of the home page offers an experiential view whereas buttons and menus provide information and transactional support, as exemplified in the website shown in Figure 2.2.

Consistency is important. One of the reasons people find menu-driven call centres so frustrating is that on the one hand you've got a human voice, while on the other hand you've got an interaction format based on lists of menu items. No restaurant waiter would simply read out the menu "press 27 for chicken tikka masala", so why should call centres?

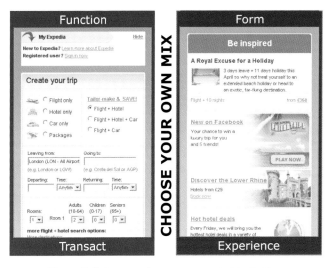

Figure 2.2 An experience surrounded by button

Design for state of mind

Ultimately, the form versus function paradox is best addressed by designing media around customers' state of mind. In some circumstances this is relatively easy to figure out and respond to, as in the funeral director's website which starts with a poem.

An emerging challenge is to devise websites that try to adapt. It is possible to ask questions to assess what customers want to do. Alternatively, using clues such as the speed of typing can attempt to assess a customer's mood; knowing the Google search terms that a user has used to arrive at your website is another pointer. The ideal is an emotionally intelligent website.

A generational perspective

The digital generation is far more likely to see digital technology as a source of entertainment. By contrast, when the toe-dippers use the internet they do so from a more functional perspective.

To recap, the main paradox here is the variety of genres of website or mobile app, and that users differ so much regarding the sort of experience they want. Some want a fast convenient trading platform whereas others want an immersive experience. The more that digital media are tuned to one type of customer the more that others can be put off.

Addressing the paradox

1. Be clear about the function of your website or application. These can be diverse – including brand awareness; trading platform; facilitating a community or social network; acting as an information resource; or providing service and support.
2. Try to predict the states of mind of your customers as they interact with your applications, and try to imagine what their motivations are. Are your customers interested in an immersive experience of your brand, or are they hoping to complete a transaction as quickly and easily as possible? Or is it a mixture of the two?
3. If there is any ambiguity – and there probably is! – look for ways of making your applications adapt. The simplest option is to have a single portal and let your customers choose which path they follow. More complicated approaches pick up on clues and adapt the experience accordingly. Consider the types of clue available, such as kind of media used; time of day; typing speed; voice characteristics and historical path through the website.
4. If your application contains "function" characteristics, think about how to make the interaction as efficient as possible. Give the option of "one-click" ordering – though this also raises the bar on security issues.
5. Conversely, where the application majors on "form", think about the "attention economy". How can you create a culturally meaningful experience for all your customers?
6. Consider how emerging technologies such as natural language input can support these objectives.
7. Look carefully at the role of mobile apps, which may span from being purely functional to using enriched media accessed via links to the web.

Notes

1. http://www.stanford.edu/group/commdept/oldstuff/srct_pages/Social-Parasocial.html
2. See their children's news site http://news.bbc.co.uk/cbbcnews/ compared with the regular news site, http://www.bbc.co.uk/news/
3. http://edition.cnn.com/ and http://edition.cnn.com/studentnews/

Paradox 3

Empowerment versus privacy

IN THE REAL WORLD, THERE'S NO SUCH THING AS A
FREE LUNCH. ON THE INTERNET THERE IS ... PROVIDED
YOU DON'T MIND EVERYONE WATCHING YOU EAT.

No free lunch

The privacy paradox is central to the internet. Part of the reason that the internet has taken off has been the availability of "free" services, supported by targeted advertising or by onward sales of data derived from these services. But many commentators believe that this information harvesting has not been through fully informed consent. Sporadic reactions against a perceived invasion of privacy are now occurring; and these merge into a wider moral panic around identity theft, leaks of official information, security and cyber crime. Conversely there are many innovations that use private data to offer genuine value to consumers. The question is how to innovate new services without crossing the line of consumers' sensibilities – how to behave appropriately.

Apply emotional intelligence to digital customer management

In the domain of psychology, knowing how to behave appropriately with different people in different situations is a key feature of emotional intelligence (EI). The challenge then is this: how, as a company, to be emotionally intelligent? How to gauge customers' (sometimes contradictory) needs correctly and to support a company image with which the customer is comfortable?

Consumers want it all ways!

The main paradoxical element of this challenge is that customers want the benefits of context sensitive communications (like the local offers provided by Vouchercloud[1]) at the same time as not wanting, for example, a record of their movements to be stored.

An emotionally intelligent customer management strategy will target customers' desires: for everything to be easy, to enable them to feel like they belong, to be offered relevant services, to enable them to feel important, to be well served, and to be able to trust the company. At the same time, the strategy should respect customers' privacy preferences: to be in control of how data about them is used – only for something for which they would approve, and that it is stored securely (see Figure 3.1).

Figure 3.1 Empowerment versus privacy

Some examples are easier to deal with than others. It is hard to argue against people wanting privacy settings across digital services and touch points, such as Facebook, to be easy to manage. But what is wrong with them being willing to accept some infringement of privacy to gain a benefit?

Two examples. It is hard to imagine an informed customer not accepting a cookie from Amazon so that they can benefit from one-click ordering next visit. Other scenarios are more ambiguous: is seeing a friend's photo of you tagged on someone else's Facebook page cool, or an infringement of privacy? The answer can depend – for example, on what the photo shows you doing, or who could see it.

Humans have simultaneous needs

Responses to Google's "Street View" encapsulates the challenge. An immense, technically brilliant feat; to photograph millions of streets around the world. And yet, in addition to accolades, it has attracted bad publicity, attempts at legal action,[2] government bans[3] and fines.[4] Reactions have varied by places, but the negative reaction has centred around privacy. Why?

To answer this, we need psychology. In our day-to-day lives we have needs of being able to act (our empowerment) and of personal space (our privacy). These norms have physical and emotional components, are in fact a combination of the two, and vary according to social and cultural context, such as: when we were born, where we live, our education, our friends and family, and so on. Any interaction we have with the outside world that is inconsistent with our own norms will feel wrong.

Humans strive to hit the right balance in the real world...

Think, for example, of the following scenarios. You enter a shop you once visited several years ago and the shopkeeper greets you like a long lost friend. You are waiting for a train and a station announcement starts describing your plans for the evening to the platform. A stranger gives you a hug as you enter the park. A long-time friend acts like they have never met you before. Strange? Why? Because the scenarios violate our norms.

... and in the same way, companies should strive for the right balance in the digital sphere

Such violations can be just as inappropriate in the digital world. A website you've never visited before greets you by your first name and asks if you would like to order something for delivery to your home address, which it already knows. Or another, from which you regularly shop, does not recognise your username or your email address. Or your data is some of that leaked by a service provider, like play.com.[5] Or you hear that Google recorded wifi data on your street when it was photographing for Street View. As a customer, you may also be perturbed – maybe more so if you recognise that once your data is available online it can be very hard to delete. In contrast, in the real world you can always avoid that strange, over-familiar shopkeeper.

This lays clear the dilemma for companies. The digital world empowers companies to target communications to their customers according to their contexts, with a high level of precision. But what are the rules that companies should follow to ensure that their digital customer management approaches do not overstep customers' comfort zones – i.e. are perceived to be appropriate? A good start to

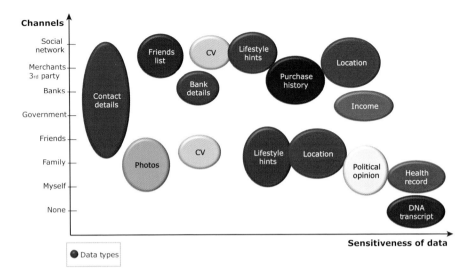

Figure 3.2 Acceptance of customers to share personal data via different channels (source BearingPoint)

answering this would be to understand what people are more concerned about sharing; that which makes them most vulnerable? Like their location, information about their wealth, happiness, health and well-being, who are their friends and foes (see Figure 3.2).

And what are the consequences of overstepping customers' comfort zones? Lower loyalty? Churn? One consequence is that customers can provide false data. Think of the UK Census in 2001, when almost 400,000 citizens declared their religion as "Jedi" (from Star Wars)! Which is better? More data – some of it wrong, or less data – none of it wrong?

Norms are personal, are influenced socially and by context, and are evolving

A further challenge in addressing the paradox is that different people have different norms, which in themselves are dynamic, and that norms change over time. Web users are now used to targeted advertising based on browsing and search behaviour. How many Gmail users realise the targeting based on email content is questionable? What is for sure is that a late adopter of email (a toe-dipper) would probably consider both, and certainly the latter, as invasive. But looking 20 years ahead, today's targeting will probably look both primitive, and discrete.

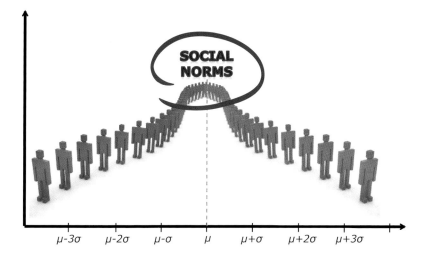

Figure 3.3 Norms are personal, they are influenced socially and by context, and are evolving (source BearingPoint)

It is important to note that while rules are defined, and can be looked up, norms – especially in new markets/domains – are much harder to read or predict. Norms are influenced by the groups people identify with. A naive customer may not know how concerned to be about their privacy, and what impacts technology can have on it. This highlights the potential role of key opinion leaders, for example as proponents for the normalisation of new patterns of customer behaviour in relation to the disclosure of personal data (see Figure 3.3).

Public awareness of privacy issues is increasing, and legislation is developing

Part of what constitutes the moving target is that public opinion can both drive and be driven by personal norms. For opinion to be triggered people need to be aware of an issue and to evaluate it. Until recently, most internet users were not aware their online behaviour was tracked, and still most do not know quite how much of it is. Times change. Awareness is increasing as a result of media coverage (for example, see the *Wall Street Journal's* 2010 feature series "What They Know", and official initiatives both in Europe and the US[6]).

Research in the UK[7] highlighted that a majority of people express concern about their personal details online, with 96% concerned that organisations do not keep their details secure; equivalent to being concerned that our friends and associates in the physical world could not be trusted with personal facts or information we chose to share with them.

To recap, the main paradox here is that customers want the benefits of context-sensitive communications while *also* wanting to maintain their privacy. The challenge for companies is how to address these conflicting needs strategically.

Addressing the paradox

1. Ensure behaviour when gathering, holding and managing customer data and privacy is appropriate to customer mindsets, for the type of product or service the company provides.
2. Understand target customers' mindsets and sensitivities with sufficient acuity to position the company in relation to: location tracking, cookies and data harvesting, and the mining of social networks.
3. Ensure company behaviour complies with legislation, and target all behaviour as appropriate – even in new markets. In new markets identify real-world equivalents and consequences of behaving inappropriately. As a simple test, check digital customer management approaches do not violate any established norms.
4. Watch and learn from others' mistakes and successes. Be wary of unintended consequences, and develop a clear company strategy and action plan to manage getting it wrong. Develop a strategy for success based on successful approaches.
5. Ensure push notifications based on context (e.g. geo-localisation) are only provided to customers who explicitly opt-in. And make sure strategy recognises and respects the limits of acceptability for push notifications (time of day, around specific events).
6. Only gather private information that brings value to end-customers, for example to support notifications or personalised offers and promotions. In this context, invest to understand which topics should be excluded from personalised services. And where possible, and more efficient to do so, target customers using generic behavioural rather than personalised approaches.
7. Use private information specialists (e.g. PayPal) or work to become a "Trusted go-between" for customers (e.g. Amazon insuring its customers in the Amazon market-place).
8. Consider investment in the deployment of key opinion leaders to normalise new behaviours (think, for example, of Stephen Fry and his Twitter feed).

Notes

1. http://www.vouchercloud.com/
2. Germany.
3. Czech Republic and Switzerland.
4. France.
5. http://www.guardian.co.uk/technology/2011/mar/22/
   play-customer-details-leaked?INTCMP=SRCH
6. With recent legislative and communications activities by the European Commission, and the Federal Trade Commission.
7. From the Information Commissioner's Office, 2010.

Paradox

Person versus persona

CALLING YOURSELF DONALD DUCK MAY BE FINE FOR CERTAIN ONLINE PURPOSES, BUT IT TENDS TO CAUSE PROBLEMS WHEN IT COMES TO CREDIT HISTORY AND DELIVERY ADDRESS.[1]

Related to the privacy paradox is our fourth paradox, which we label Person versus Persona. Its central concern is how much companies require their customers to disclose, or reveal, of their real identity. A "person" is someone who has disclosed key aspects of their identity to the company whereas a "persona" is a partial or inaccurate image of someone who has not disclosed key aspects of their identity, as illustrated in Figure 4.1.

Using the same terminology as we did for our privacy paradox, the main paradoxical element of this challenge is that customers simultaneously want the benefits of personalised and targeted communications, while wanting only to reveal or disclose a subset or partial image of the information that would enable full personalisation – or to remain anonymous.

Of course, in most cases the dichotomy is not so extreme, but at the core of the paradox is a gap between what companies want or need their customers to reveal and what customers feel comfortable or willing to reveal. There are therefore two potential approaches to bridging the gap: recognising that withholding disclosure is OK, and designing business processes around more anonymity, or encouraging customers to disclose more private information, of the type(s) towards the right side of Figure 4.1.

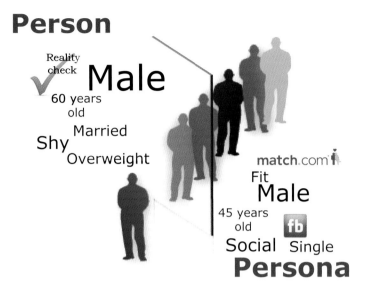

Figure 4.1 Customers can benefit by controlling what they reveal

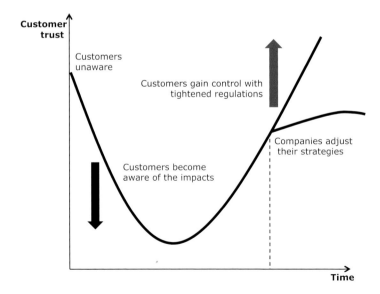

Figure 4.2 Companies adjust their strategies to build customer trust (source BearingPoint)

Around both these approaches there is a fundamental need – to support the development of a trusting relationship with your customers.

Companies should communicate to customers the benefits of making themselves known

To develop strategies that address the paradox, it is first useful to make explicit the positives from the customer perspective of being known (a person) or somewhat known (a persona). In relation to their identities online, customers gain many benefits from revealing their identities, enabling them to be known to companies (see Figure 4.2). So these benefits should be clarified to customers.

First, and most generic, are those related to ease of interaction and transaction (e.g. Amazon's one-click ordering) to simplify a customer's life. To enable this benefit requires a customer to be recognised by providers of services and products. A good example is that if you disclose your phone number to British Airways, you will receive a travel reminder by SMS, with a link to a map of the terminal, travel tips to get to the airport and a link to buy transport tickets online. A further level of associated benefits can also be communicated to customers – for example that quicker, easier shopping can lead to more time for you to relax (or have fun, spend time with the family, etc.)

A second group of benefits to customers who allow themselves to be known relates to a company's ability to target appropriate offers and deals. Good examples are mechanisms such as Amazon's personalised recommendations based on previous purchase behaviours, or on their (less personalised) pre-purchase advice (e.g., X% of people who viewed this product eventually purchased "product y"), or the targeted adverts received by Gmail users.

A third group of benefits relates to the psychology of group membership, literally helping customers feel that they belong within a company's community or family. The more strongly customers identify themselves with a company, the more loyal they are likely to be and the less likely they will be to churn to the services of a competitor. The inclusion of social media within a company website – like amazon.com – does exactly this. Examples of customers disclosing their person for the benefit of being part of a community are plentiful – think of Special K's online diet club (at www.myspecialk.co.uk), where people share very personal information in order to benefit from community support, recipes and so on.

Customers can benefit by controlling what they reveal: Companies who help them do it will gain

Just as customers can receive enhanced offers by revealing their identities, at other times and in other contexts those benefits might be outweighed by more important needs and considerations.

One of the most referred to appeals of the internet is that users can be anonymous online. Anonymity, real or perceived, can enable internet users to accomplish a whole range of goals online associated with wish fulfilment. Examples are many, and range from playing the role of a person of different sex or age in an online gaming context, to being able to express feelings that may not be socially desirable, or politically correct – or which for any reason a person may not be confident to say publicly.[2] Some industry leaders, Zuckerberg included, think anonymity will only have a limited (if any) role online in the future. But don't forget that companies can leverage customers' preference for anonymity by asking for anonymous feedback for service or product improvements – in order to get more honest answers.

Companies can show they understand customer concerns, and invest in enabling customer trust

A second set of benefits to customers of partial anonymity, or partial disclosure, relates to managing the consequences of disclosure. For example, why is it worth it for consumers to create online aliases, or manage multiple email accounts?

A simple reason is to avoid spam clogging up a valued communications channel. Promise your customers that they will never receive an unsolicited communication from you, and that you will never pass their details to any third party, and help them to trust your commitment to that, and increase the likelihood that they will disclose more to you about their person. Windows Live's recent launch of email aliases to link to one head email account is evidence of the increasing popularity of customers managing their identities. And it will give MSN the ability to aggregate online behavioural data from several Windows Live aliases. Windows Live is fulfilling a customer need, and gaining a new insight tool – through the same application.

A second reason might be to avoid risking loss of privacy of personal information. So, if your play.com profile was to an extent fictitious (or at least partial) you would have been less worried about play.com's data centres having been hacked into in March 2011. So don't forget to check how your behaviour is likely to be perceived and felt by your customers. Just like in friendships, the more trustworthy you are the more likely people are to trust you.

Customer concerns about privacy may be rational

A third reason? You'll no doubt have lost count of the number of press articles pointing out that putting too much information about your social life online can influence how you are perceived in the workplace. The impact has been discussed extensively in relation to recruitment, where a preferred applicant was ruled out of the running as a result of the recruiter spotting a "wrong" photo on the applicant's Facebook page.

So what? Recognise that customers are actually becoming increasingly smart at managing their disclosure. They either have to not reveal anything interesting – in which case they are missing out on some of the fun and benefits of social media – or they have to manage multiple identities. It is for this reason that not many people have the same profile picture on LinkedIn as on Facebook.

Related to being able to manage identities, a final theme to mention here is one about which the public is becoming increasingly aware. Once personal information is revealed online, it is very hard (if not impossible) to delete it. Effectively, people's digital footprints are almost permanent. As more people realise this, for example through media literacy activities like those of Kidsmart,[3] it is important that companies are sensitive to customers' preferences for anonymity. And anonymous customers can still be lucrative, if payment mechanisms are implemented to support anonymous transactions – for example pre-paid credit cards or other pre-pay online payment systems.

To recap, the main paradox here is that customers simultaneously want the benefits of personalised and targeted communications, while wanting only to reveal or disclose a subset or partial image of the information that would enable full personalisation – or to remain anonymous. The challenge for companies is how to address these conflicting preferences.

Addressing the paradox

1. Understand customers' mindsets and sensitivities to inform strategy in relation to identifying customers.
2. Conduct an honest appraisal of the context in which the strategy is being applied. Per service/product, conduct cost-benefit and/or SWOT analyses of different customer identification options for different types of customer.
3. Within these analyses include the costs and benefits of capturing, storing and aggregating data on customers, and target customers. Other aspects to consider relate to the extent to which you already (or should) offer localised (to a country or region) or personalised (to a person or persona) products and services.

4. Agree an explicit rationale to drive the level of customer identification needed. Develop this rationale commercially. For example, it is more likely to be worth identifying in more depth high-value than low-value/one-off customers. Target the level of identification your rationale specifies, and no more.

5. Where anonymous transactions are a possibility, enable and support them.

6. Invest in being a trusted partner of your customer – a guardian of their privacy, regardless of how much they choose to reveal.

7. Consider ways of differentiating your company in this domain. For example, allow customers to request the full deletion of all data your company systems hold.

8. Recognise the potential for a company to have its own personas to create interactions with customers' persons and personas and/or to manage fictitious personas to influence online reputation (like the US military do![4]).

Notes

1. Unless you live at 1313 Webfoot Walk in Duckburg, Calisota.
2. http://www.networkworld.com/community/
   blog/4chan-founder-moot-anonymity-authenticity-zuc
3. http://www.kidsmart.org.uk/digitalfootprints/
4. http://www.guardian.co.uk/technology/2011/mar/17/
   us-spy-operation-social-networks?INTCMP=SRCH

 *Paradox*

Choice versus recommendation

I WANT TO DECIDE. DO YOU HAVE ANY SUGGESTIONS?

Amazon has 34 million books in its catalogue[1] – far too many to browse. If book selection were through title search alone, there would be no equivalent of the traditional browsing experience. So Amazon has sophisticated ways of recommending books to its customers, based on both individual and statistical information. But Amazon's ability to provide recommendations, as well as the execution of its policy, is extremely sophisticated. Customers must trust Amazon enough to allow the company to make recommendations, and must not feel affronted by the recommendations that are made – even if they are made on the basis of purchases of presents.

The fundamental paradox here relates to humans wanting to feel that they have freedom of choice at the same time as feeling nervous about making the right decision – and so wanting pointers, reassurance or recommendations (see Figure 5.1).

Customers simultaneously want to feel autonomous, while needing to be guided. So this fifth paradox is related to our earlier ones: companies' positioning and strategy with regard to privacy and level of disclosure required of customers have implications regarding room for manoeuvre here.

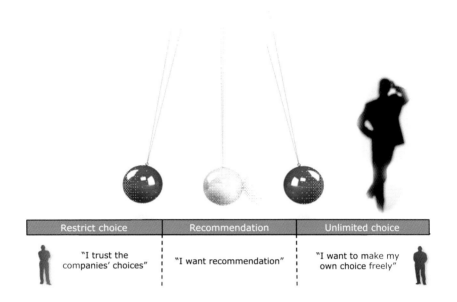

Figure 5.1 Choice versus recommendation (source BearingPoint)

Customers want to *feel* independent and unique

The challenge for companies is how to offer an appropriate range of products or services to their customers, to address their customers' needs, and present that range in a way that helps customers make transactions they will be happy with. From a psychological perspective, companies need to be aware that a transaction about which a customer will be happy will need to have struck a balance between impeding their customers' sense of autonomy, and confusing customers with choice. The target is a sweet range, a balance, which will vary for different types of products and services, and customer. Again, addressing the paradox requires emotional intelligence – to accurately gauge customers' mindsets and needs, and respond appropriately.

Querying the motive behind a recommendation can be rational

It is easy to understand a range of drivers to customers wanting choice, and being wary of recommendations. For example, customers could be aware that any recommendation may be inaccurate – it may not take account of the most relevant information about a customer. Others may question whether a recommendation is best for them as customers, or for the seller – providing the best margin. A recommendation that serves to maximise profit for a seller is great, but acknowledging that this is a possibility can be a rational driver to customers wanting to search a full product range for themselves – to check whether another solution might better meet their needs, more cheaply.

Note that the cost to a customer of double checking a recommendation online is much lower than in the physical world – whether that means checking other online reviews, using other price comparison tools or polling friends quickly online (e.g. on Facebook or Twitter, or via email). Facebook's Questions is a recognition of this trend.[2]

Also, recommendations may be relevant in some contexts but not in others. The relevance of recommendations to the same customer can vary dependent on their mood, what sort of day they've been having, how close they are to pay day and so on. And in different contexts, customers may want recommendations focused on specific characteristics. When searching for a rare purchase, such as a home entertainment system, I may want to prioritise quality over price; when buying regular consumables price may be my priority.

So, given this variety, why even think of recommendations?

Customers really do need recommendations

On what basis should a customer make a decision about which to buy of hundreds of mobile phones, or TVs? It could be on the basis of any of a range of variables: peer recommendation, price, functionality, brand, colour, design, look and feel, who the typical user of the product is and so on.

In the physical world, customers could always visit a store and explore, and when they felt the need – for example, for reassurance – they could ask a salesperson's advice. Myriad mystery shopping studies, and customer experiences, have shown that salespeople are not always available when needed, and when they are they may not have at hand the information the customer needs. Worse, the salesperson might be biased – promoting a specific product for commercial reasons.

In the digital world, customers can search for reviews, recommendations and advice from a very large pool of trusted sites, where the community of reviewers is big, or composed of people they know. Foursquare's success is an excellent example of the appeal of recommendations about specific places from friends.

Transparent information enables informed choices; too much can paralyse

In order to make any decision on a rational basis, people need transparent information about different choices. Such information has three features. First, it must be meaningful – using relevant product characteristics. Secondly, it must be accurate and honest. And thirdly, it must be comparable. Comparability is also affected by how many choices are available, and how much information is available about each.

As Barry Shwartz points out in *The Paradox of Choice*,[3] too much choice can reduce satisfaction and render decisions impossible. Similarly, too much information can hinder transparency. Ofgem (the UK energy regulator) recently criticised the bewildering number of tariffs as being against the public interest.[4] In this context, it is clear to see that an ongoing role for recommendations is guaranteed.

Recommendations have diverse roles

So what roles do recommendations fulfil for customers? First, and most general, is that of supporting a decision from a wide range of potentially suitable options. The higher the perceived complexity of the offer, risk of making the wrong decision, or cost of the decision, the more important is this role. A good example is Cartier's website, designed to enable visitors to explore a wide and varied catalogue in a designed atmosphere (set by music and image), and offering the Cartier Guide for expert advice and suggestions.

Secondly is the role of reassuring customers that they are making the right decision. This role is observable in relation to big ticket purchases, to which customers have higher emotional engagement. Here, lengthy, immersive experiences are optimal. The Nissan website is a good example – it provides an engaging, playful experience using video, 3D models, goodies and games.

Thirdly is the role of advising in relation to a product that requires expertise to enjoy. A good example is in relation to online wine stores: wineandco.com is designed to guide both novices and experts through a huge online catalogue. Visitors can search for wines by price, region or variety, and several big name wines are easy to navigate to on the home page – to guide visitors to best sellers. Experts can use advanced search options, directly entering keywords and other detailed attributes.

For any role to be fulfilled effectively depends on visitors trusting the source. Just like in the real world, where shoppers ask a salesperson for advice, customers are interested in the content and also in the dialogue. Shoppers can be more inclined to buy when there is a social dimension to the shopping experience. So how can this be reproduced in digital? The answer lies in adding social engagement to the vast volume of information available online, coupling recommendations with more personalised advice – and, for example, offering more socially engaging channels when it appears an online shopper might abandon the process (e.g. to chat with an avatar or webcam with a call centre agent).

It is easier to take recommendations and reassurance from trusted sources

It makes sense for a person to better take a selection recommendation from a friend than from an unknown entity. So what characterises a friend? The psychological literature would suggest someone who you trust, can be open with and is open with you, who is honest and fair, has your best interests at heart, and is like you in respects you consider important. Companies wanting their recommendations to be valued, and heard, should strive for these characteristics.

This highlights again the virtuous circle of trust in the digital world. To make a good recommendation requires the recommender to know the customer's needs, and for the customer to reveal their needs they need to trust the recommender. A recommendation from someone you know for a product meeting your needs is much more likely to feel like a recommendation than like someone trying to sell you something. The increasing popularity and impact of social media among many segments suggests a growing role for social media contacts as recommenders, or commenters on decisions. This crowd-sourcing approach to recommendations also addresses people's preference to take recommendations from friends. The online nature of such engagement enables it to be updated in real time, reflecting most current views. And if companies enable customers to provide feedback, the review system should also be open to suppliers to respond.

Celebrity or expert status matters

A final psychological insight to note relevant to choice and recommendation relates to people wanting to feel (and be) a little unique, but generally acting as a herd. It's not for fun that Amazon tells customers browsing its site that X% of people who viewed this product went ahead and bought it. It is an example of what psychologists call "normative cueing" – encouraging customers to behave in a way a group behaves. And behaving in the way someone with a desirable identity behaves is also the basis of expert or celebrity endorsement of a product or service.

Customers are confused by having too many choices

Understand customers through 4 key questions			
What?	**When?**	**Who?**	**How?**
Product/service/content	Situation/time of delay	Client	Chanel/device

Recommendation/Strategy

Figure 5.2 Companies need to define their strategy:
Let the customer choose or guide through recommendations (source BearingPoint)

So the challenge for recommendations is this. Customers are confident when trusted groups give them advice, but at the same time they do not want to be like all the sheep in the herd. How can companies help customers be that little bit different, while generally following the trend (see Figure 5.2)?

The domain of this paradox is one in which companies really can innovate, and benefit from getting it right – being seen as a better friend of the customer; trusted, loyal and valued.

To recap, the main paradox here is that customers want to feel that they have freedom of choice at the same time as feeling nervous about making the right decision – and so needing pointers, reassurance or recommendations. The challenge for companies is how to address both needs simultaneously.

Addressing the paradox

1. Identify a general recommendation strategy: (a) artificially limit choice to "blockbuster" products, or (b) offer a large range ("long tail"), and provide tools to help customers choose what is right for them. The latter is more typical in the digital world.

2. Understand customers' mindsets, sensitivities, goals and behaviours in depth in order to optimise the quality of customers' experience(s) of interaction in search/recommendation tools.

3. Offer search and recommendation tools to match customer preferences from a range of approaches available (consider: explicit search, implicit behavioural, promotional, celebrity/expert endorsement, peer review and crowd-sourcing, and serendipity – "feeling lucky?").

4. Innovate in recommendation solutions – for example, provide digital recommendations in physical space: access reviews on mobile devices, contact friends/family for advice/co-shopping with Skype and webcam, provide bespoke advertisements about the benefits products can offer.

5. Recognise what makes people give recommendations in real life – to self-identify as important, helpful, an expert, a player, connected – and emulate that.

6. Ensure there is an explicit rationale for when to recommend (e.g. to reassure about high price/big decision or to help a customer to enjoy a product/service) and when not to (e.g. for repeat purchases or for low-value/low emotional engagement transactions).

7. Enable customers to trust a company making a recommendation. Do not make wrong recommendations: just like in real life, trust broken is very hard to win back!

Notes

1. As at March 2011.
2. http://blog.facebook.com/blog.php?post=10150110059982131
3. Schwartz, B. (2003). *The Paradox of Choice: Why More Is Less*, Ecco.
4. http://www.ofgem.gov.uk/Media/PressRel/Documents1/RMRFinal%20Final.pdf

TRANSACT
efficiently

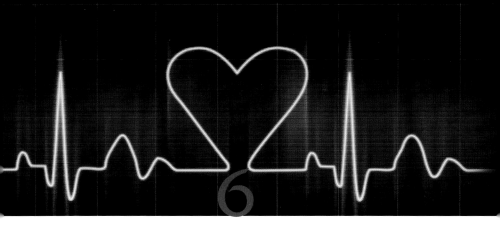

Put mobile at the heart of your digital strategy

SALES AND DIRECT MARKETING CHANNEL, PAYMENT TERMINAL OR EVEN BUSINESS MANAGEMENT TOOL, THE MOBILE PHONE IS THE NEW "SWISS ARMY KNIFE". IT IS ALSO THE LINK BETWEEN CONTACT CHANNELS IN THE PURCHASE LIFE CYCLE.

Shopping in the smartphone era has been revolutionised. Since it arrived, consumers have been demanding more of their mobile phone. Being able to connect to the internet anywhere is now a prerequisite. Not only Apple but also the whole industry has moved into a new era since smartphones came onto the scene. Thanks to their intuitive interfaces, large screens and compatibility with 3G, GPS, wifi and Bluetooth protocols, they offer a completely new web experience. The figures confirm their success: 71 million Europeans surf the net at least one hour a day on their mobiles.[1] Another sign: mobile internet adoption is happening much more quickly than PC internet adoption. Nowadays, more internet pages are read on mobiles than on computers, and this trend shows no sign of slowing down. It took the Blackberry 300 days to reach 1 million units sold; for the iPhone, 74 days only were necessary; and for the iPad the milestone was reached in a record 24 days![2] Morgan Stanley predicts that, by 2012, the total number of shipped smartphones worldwide will outgrow the total number of shipped PCs.[3]

Assisted by the extension of communications networks and the inventiveness of application developers, the mobile has become a channel in its own right. Sales, marketing and service interactions are going mobile. Following the music and gaming sectors, retail is going mobile. "Pure players" such as Amazon and eBay have developed sophisticated buying experiences on the mobile for all kinds of products. Retailers operating chains of stores are getting a taste for it too. Clothing brand Next has launched a pioneering mobile app that provides style ideas, store locator services and a slick mobile shopping experience.

From voice to data

The explosion of fun and functional mobile apps has also provided a new collaborative and interactive platform for building brand awareness. The most popular app in the UK in 2009 (more than 1 million downloads) simulated drinking a pint of beer. Known as Carling's iPint, not surprisingly people share it with their family, colleagues and friends! The Zippo app is another blockbuster. With more that 6 million downloads, it displays a cigarette lighter with a flame that is so realistic that people use it at parties and concerts. These two stories prove that brand communication on the mobile often plays on the point where emotion meets the community dimension.

But the mobile phone is also a serious medium! Companies develop free functional apps. Automotive manufacturer BMW recently launched M Power, which measures the acceleration of any make of car. Mobile marketing brings the beginning of a new era of permissive marketing enhanced by GPS, which combines location, relevance and immediacy. But sophisticated analytics and decision tools will never drive the same level of return as offers pulled by consumers who are opting in to receive relevant vouchers and discounts. Stored on their phones or triggered as they approach a store, mobile vouchers will become a convenient and compelling marketing tool. With the increased transparency provided by the price comparison sites, the use of high-value time-limited and location targeted offers will take direct marketing to a new level and must be integrated into the design of loyalty programmes.

Mobile self-service

For business, the smartphone can also become a low-cost self-service channel as transactions are delegated to consumers. Airlines, banks and insurance companies were the first to do this. British Airways and Lufthansa have developed self-check-in procedures that can handle upgrades. Motor insurer Geico makes use of the mobile phone's camera. Its customers can file claims in the form of a video filmed at the scene of the accident. In the banking sector, account management is moving to the smartphone. More than 3.5 million Bank of America customers use it. As well as providing real-time connection to finances enabling payments and transfers on the move, another US bank has developed a free, secure and easy app allowing consumers to deposit cheques instantly wherever they are, merely by taking a photo of it. The trend has reached Europe where 14% of British and 9% of French and Germans carry out banking services on their mobiles.

The first contact channel that enables a continuous conversation

The mobile phone is a ubiquitous tool that is breaking down the barriers between conventional channels. From a smartphone in a shop, a consumer can connect to social networks and get advice from friends when making a purchase. The mobile can also enhance the store experience by providing in-store navigation, companion products, accessories, recipes, advice and prices as well as competitor comparisons. It can also be used to pay. Barclaycard has launched a contactless payment solution in partnership with Orange.[4]

The growth of mobile internet has created a new indispensible channel. Companies must embrace mobile to optimise marketing return, create a convenient shopping experience that drives conversion and cross-sell, and equips customers for self-service. It is disrupting the role and purpose of our traditional channels and is reshaping the customer purchase life cycle. Rather than a series of channel interactions, mobile is enabling a continuous conversation from awareness to purchase, and is becoming the main tool for experiencing and navigating our existing channels.

So how should companies respond to the rise of mobile? The customer journey and experience must be redefined to facilitate this seamless and continuous conversation. To achieve this, from optimising mobile integration to enhancing face-to-face interactions, the role and purpose of each channel must be reassessed. Operations will also be impacted. Companies will be forced to simplify their product and service offerings and build the organisation around customers to equip them to execute effectively throughout the dynamic and mobile customer journey. Finally, a step change in online and mobile channel information and technology capability is required.

Customer expectations on quality, availability and usability of services, products and interactions have increased dramatically. Bolt-ons to existing channels will not fulfil these expectations, but rather turn users away to niche players who excel in providing these channels.

Companies who rise to the mobile challenge and respond to the customer requirement for ubiquitous connectivity will grow engagement, advocacy and revenue as the customer relationship becomes a continuous conversation.

Notes

1. The European Interactive Advertising Association (2010). *New Decade Heralds The Age Of Digital Mobility*.
2. Morgan Stanley Research (2010). *Internet Trends*.
3. Ibid.
4. Barclaycard (2010). *Barclaycard to Launch Contactless Mobile Payments with Orange*, press release, 4 March.

Innovate through new touch points

CUSTOMERS ARE TAKING ADVANTAGE OF A WIDE RANGE OF
TOUCH POINTS, COMBINING CUSTOMER-DRIVEN EXPERIENCES
AND MORE TRADITIONAL COMPANY MARKETING OPERATIONS,
REVEALING AN INTRICATE PURCHASING JOURNEY.

No longer niche markets, digital assets are taking a growing share in the purchase funnel, putting pressure on e-business and customer management executives to enrich their strategy with new touch point sequences. This assessment needs obviously to be completed using a proper digital maturity model that goes beyond social networks penetration in the targeted country.

Do consumer-driven touch points favour more investment in digital channels?

In today's purchase journey, consumer-driven marketing operations are increasingly important as customers take control of the process and actively "search and retrieve" information helpful in decision making. Consumer-driven touch points – where consumers are reaching out for information, talking with their friends, and via internet searches and community feedback on third-party sites – are taking the leading role over firm or brand-driven touch points.

According to a recent multi-channel study by Forrester (September 2010), search engines are now the third most commonly used method of learning about a considered purchase (after physical stores and relatives). Among daily mobile internet users – nearly 12 million people in Europe – one-third have already researched products or services using the mobile internet, and 18% of them have compared prices on a mobile device while in a shop.

These usages are indicative of the potential for digital distribution channels and their potential impact on the purchase funnel, whether or not transactions are being processed online. Also, mobile e-commerce usages are entering a more mature phase on the European market as major companies deploy mass market application on these channels (e.g. Amtrack ticketing iPhone applications, Carrefour optimising its shopping site for mobile on m.carrefour.fr, or Sephora allowing customers to use their mobile phone to access reviews in the store).

One of the main challenges to maintaining this strong performance lies in combining these digital assets such as websites and mobile applications (dedicated to products or comparison sites) with programs to foster word-of-mouth, and targeted advertising platforms to deliver a consistent approach. Even if one-third of the touch points involve firm-driven assets marketing teams should anticipate and dedicate more resources to balance push-mode communication and firm-driven messages toward consumer-driven touch points.

Emerging digital sequences

The emergence of increasingly well-informed consumers implies a need to update and refine touch point sequences combining consumer and firm-driven assets. Also, as usages vary depending on users' typology (mainly based on their age), the idea of touch point typology is gaining ground. The generation of "digital transitioners" aged from 25-45 are seen as "smartshoppers" according to a recent Orange Labs consumer panel. Influenced by horizontal organisational trends such as active evaluation (ratings, specialised blogs) or community sharing on social networks, they attach value to brands investing in original digital campaigns using their new familiar touch points and a rewarding creative process. As emphasised in Chapters 1-5, generational differences characterise openness to engaging with digital and corresponding digital sequences on the purchasing journey.

About one in eight European net users with a mobile phone use mobile banking today – with SMS account alerts being the most common type. They are early adopters who use mobile banking as a complement to other channels like (PC-based) online banking, mainly to check balances and view recent transactions. Today's iPhone and BlackBerry users are already nearly three times as likely to use mobile banking as other mobile phone users. In France most banks now have application shops (like Apple Store) offering personal finance applications as a way of attracting prospective customers (like Crédit Agricole's "Mon budget"). While "digital transitioners" will move progressively to take up these new offers as they use complementary channels to complete their journey, the "digital generation" under 25 will shift easily to a pure digital journey.

The luxury sector, meanwhile, has made iPhone and iPad its own by launching mobile applications such as virtual catalogue, store locator (e.g. geo-location of shops) and even virtual trying on clothes.

In-store experience using iPad tablets gives clients access to extra-catalogue premium products. This new kind of sequence implies dynamic interactions between physical and digital touch points. The client has to come physically into the store but a dedicated sales representative will interact with them via digital tablets. Interestingly, these "digital friends" appear both as third-party players for decision making in physical stores with vendors as well as classical information tools (comparison portal), using for instance web applications or a mobile portal in the purchase funnel.

In the airline sector, frequent flyers can already buy tickets, check flights and get boarding passes via smartphone. According to Jupiter Research's *2010 Mobile Ticketing* report, about 15 billion boarding passes will be sold by 2014. This new sequence, giving more agility and mobility, is progressively replacing the old one that began with the ticket purchase (online or not), followed by the boarding pass print (if bought online) with a risk of the ticket being lost.

In the rail sector, a French company has adopted new applications for interactive terminals in its agencies, allowing customers to buy and/or to print train tickets. The main benefit for the end-user comes from the complementarity approach, involving an "in station" terminal and an online experience.

Far from being homogenous, emerging digital sequences are nevertheless founded on a combination of key factors (age profile, consumer-driven touch point influence, synergies with physical store and technology innovations) allowing proper design for marketing planning purposes and consistency for the brand.

Mobiles: The pre-eminent touch point in multi-channel strategies

As widely publicised by various digital studies, more and more clients will be using their mobile phones to access services and perform various pre-purchase actions on brands or third-party websites. A range of factors explain this trend, like smartphones becoming the norm; all-you-can-eat data plans; and more personalised content delivered by brands to attract customers. These developments in the relevant touch points not only represent a challenge in extending the brand and services' ecosystem but are also about arranging the right sequences as mobile usages introduce changes in the information expected at each stage of the purchase funnel.

The pre-eminence of the mobile as the principal touch point for digital sequences by customers has been boosted by technological innovations. Augmented reality, geo-location, geo-fencing and soon their combination with social networks will contribute to providing a new seamless mobile experience to customers, and opportunities for the brand to renew client intimacy.

Mobile devices as extensions of the self

The new digital channels are becoming more complex and marketing teams must adapt their mix of channels, taking full advantages of potential intimacy and real-time message delivery, especially on mobile devices considered by Turkle as "extensions of the self". As mentioned earlier, the challenge lies in identifying the optimal sequence from each digital generation and the imperative is to provide a consistent and ideally seamless customer journey.

As the sequences are modified with an increasing sense of reactivity (consumer-driven touch points) and time efficiency (real-time expectations), purchases will accelerate and involve more social interactions, generating new information expectations (real-time updates on mobile phones, personal account personalisation on brand portals) and leading to a better conversion rate and brand recognition on digital channels.

Learn from emerging markets: Mobile services

MOBILE TRANSACTIONS USED TO BE A SYNONYM FOR EITHER MOBILE BANKING OR MOBILE PAYMENTS AND MONEY TRANSFERS. WHILE THIS IS STILL THE CASE, SUCH TRANSACTIONS TODAY EMBRACE MANY OTHER APPLICATIONS.

Technologies such as barcode and NFC (Near Field Communication) ultra-localisation, combined with WiFi, 3G or LTE network coverage are enabling new mobile transaction concepts such as ubiquity shopping and smart couponing. Mobile transactions today therefore must be understood in a broader sense, from shopping to customer service via payment and access controls, representing a new purchasing and user experience that removes the frontier between the physical and digital worlds.

The year when m-commerce exploded

"The year when m-commerce exploded has already happened – it was 2009", says Benoît Corbin, CEO of the French Mobile Marketing Association. This statement is confirmed by e-commerce giants such as eBay (hitting nearly $2 billion in m-commerce sales worldwide in 2010) as well as numbers and projections on mobile payments worldwide (source IE Market Research

Corporation) which also demonstrate that mobile transactions have ceased to be an emerging concept:

- The number of m-payment users should increase from $351 million in 2009 to $1.09 billion in 2014, with payments rising from $37.4 billion to $1.13 trillion.
- $7.4 billion of merchandise is sold via mobile phones, for an average transaction value of $13; it should increase to $224 billion in 2014 with an average basket of just over $17.
- Mobile money transfers should reach $148 billion in 2014.

Note that these numbers encompass two types of mobile transaction:

- transactions carried out on the mobile internet; and
- transactions performed using the "intelligence" of mobile devices to buy from non-web sources, involving a transactional model based on operator's invoice, SMS/SMS+, RFID/NFC, etc.

In this chapter we will focus on the second kind of mobile transaction. Predicting and understanding major mobile transaction trends is far from easy. How should enterprises evolve to offer new products and services, and to interact differently with customers, and at what pace? There is no single answer because local needs and market maturity have an even stronger influence for mobile transactions than for traditional internet transactions.

Mobile transactions for mass-services in developed markets

We have entered the third wave of mobile transactions in developed markets, leveraging phone functions from convenience service to brand new experience:

- The first wave was mainly about buying digital content to play games or to personalise the mobile phone (ringtones, logos, adult content, voting and so forth), with payment through operator's invoice or SMS systems.
- The second wave, predominating in recent times, saw mobile transactions venturing into the real world, providing secure, convenient services that did not generate revenues. These service were adapted to the characteristics of most of the developed countries – i.e. highly urban, with massive transportation systems and special emphasis on entertainment, involving m-parking, m-check-in for planes (Air France/KLM, Delta, AirAsia, Qantas, Virgin, etc.), m-ticketing in trains (volumes doubled in 2010) or for shows (movies, sports, concerts and theatre plays).
- The third wave is now really mixing the digital and real worlds... and it is just the beginning!

Not surprisingly, the new paradigm introduced by the iPhone in 2008 has had a tremendous influence on the development of m-transactions in developed markets. Smartphones already account for 31% of the installed base of mobile phones in the five major European countries (Italy, France, Germany, Spain, UK) and the USA in 2010 (source *Le Monde Informatique*, January 2011) and represent 37% of sales in these markets (Gartner, IDC). Not only do today's smartphones provide an intuitive interface, thus removing a huge barrier to mobile transactions, but the use of mobile apps has also introduced a decisive shift in consumer attitudes. As Jamie Wells (Director of Global Trade Marketing at Microsoft Mobile Advertising) puts it: "Consumers are getting over the trust barriers associated with mobile commerce."

This has of course materialised in the digital world: especially skyrocketing numbers of applications sold due to the extreme popularity of games on social networks for instance, generating a global turnover of $1.7 billion in 2010 and potentially $38 billion in 2014, including $8 billion for tablets alone (source Forrester report, February 2011). But this has also impacted mobile transactions in the offline world, leading key players of the mobile transactions ecosystem to cooperate to answer customer needs, the best example being telco operators and banks now deciding to develop mobile payments in Europe.

Another decisive shift should happen in 2011: mobile phone builders will almost systematically include NFC (Near Field Communication) functionalities in their phones, says Mary Carol Harris, VP of Visa Europe in charge of innovation. NFC chips enable people to perform mobile transactions in a very simple manner, just by placing the mobile phone a few centimetres away from an NFC terminal or an NFC tag in a magazine or on a poster. Usages are countless, and many are already popular in Japan and in South Korea, including payments in stores, access control to buses or trains, mobile ticketing for events and coupon redeeming in stores. NFC could actually revolutionise the way people shop – for instance, smart posters with NFC tags could create immediate interactions between potential buyers and their prospective purchases. By 2013, Informa believes approximately 11% of mobile phones will be NFC-enabled, and the telco operator Orange has announced it expects that over 50% of its smartphones sold in Europe to be NFC-enabled by as early as in 2011. However, retailers must invest in additional infrastructure, because they must be equipped with NFC-enabled terminals. As evidence of the growing appetite of major players in the mobile space for e-payments, Google is said to be preparing the launch of an NFC payment service, with pilots in the cities of San Francisco and New York in 2011, including installation of NFC terminals at points of sale.

Other new trends fuelling the growth of mobile transactions include:

• The extreme simplification of user experience brought about by intuitive interfaces. Your phone "speaks" young people's new language of video and photo so, on Amazon, iPhone users who download a specific app may capture an image with their camera and the Amazon system responds with a link to the closest match in its database, plus an option to buy the item at once.

• The growing popularity of geo-localised social networks, enabling for example more contextual marketing campaigns. Followers from a brand on a social network would for instance receive a coupon if they find themselves a short distance from a physical point of sale for that brand, combined with flash sales in that store.

Overall, mobile transactions in developed markets are mostly based on B2B2C models, whereas emerging countries are developing more B2C or C2C types of models.

Mobile transactions for mass-services in emerging markets

Mobile transactions in emerging markets are mostly about leveraging the fact that almost everyone in these countries has a mobile phone – even a simple one with only voice and SMS functions. Mobile transactions are used to offer services that are otherwise not accessible in these countries because of poor infrastructure (banking infrastructure, computers and internet access, or even landline phone). Most revealing examples are m-payment and m-banking services, which have started to become widespread in many African countries and in Asia. Perhaps the most striking illustration is M-PESA in Kenya, which carries 30% of the country's financial flows on basic phones with SMS user experience. Over 50% of the Kenyan adult population use the service to send money to far-flung relatives, in order to pay for shopping, utility bills, or even a night on the tiles and a taxi ride home (source BBC, November 22nd 2010). These services can also be used to top up from abroad the mobile pre-paid cards of family members and relatives. All in all, it is about simplifying day-to-day lives: in these countries, cash, which requires a physical interaction, is replaced by m-payments that can be managed remotely.

Other examples show that simple SMS-based mobile transactions can play a decisive role in agricultural production, as with the Raita Mitra module in India, which enables close management of water and electricity supply. This box is connected to a water pump, and sends an SMS to the farmer when there is enough water to operate the pump. The farmer then sends back an SMS containing a basic code (e.g. ON) to start the pump and irrigate the field, and only has to send another SMS (e.g. STP) to stop it. There are other interesting examples showing that mobile transactions with simple phones can greatly compensate for the lack of business and technical infrastructure.

In the same manner, mobile transactions may be used in both emerging and developed markets to simplify customers' lives and ease service delivery for proximity businesses, thanks to dematerialisation.

Mobile transactions for services and proximity businesses

Service businesses have already understood that mobile devices can help them give their customers a better service and streamline their processes, as shown by already widespread PDA order taking in restaurants. Most enterprises using Personal Digital Assistants for their field force (potentially with embedded barcode scanning, RFID reader, mini-printer and scanner) estimate that they generate substantial productivity gains, but also enhance the company's image.

Today, new technology on mobile devices, including but not limited to smartphones, enables further developments of simpler and enhanced service delivery, both from a consumer and an enterprise standpoint. Here are some interesting examples:

- Based on crypto-acoustics, Openways technology replaces room keys for hotels by offering a mobile application that opens customer room doors in a simple and secure manner with a sound. Customers have a convenient and time-saving check-in process, and employees also save time and may therefore concentrate on more added-value service to customers.

- The same principles could be applied by car rental business, with customers using a mobile phone code to unlock their cars, along with supporting vehicle localisation. In this case again, both the customer and the enterprise would gain from the service: customers basically save time in their journey, while the car rental firm optimises its processes and may reduce on-site teams at pick-up sites.

- The mailman could soon be in a closer relationship with customers, thanks to a website coupled with a mailman PDA. A suitable date and time for delivery of registered letters will be supplied by recipients, which would make life easier for recipients (no need to go to the post office in case of a missed delivery) and will obviously help the postal service (optimisation of delivery, geo-localised alerts to ease mailman work, reduction of the number of items awaiting delivery, etc.).

- Kayentis digital pen and smart paper technology enables service organisations – for instance healthcare and life science professionals – to fill in a form by hand, while a camera embedded in the pen captures the handwritten data and transmits it in real time via a USB or a Bluetooth connection. Simple data collection can thus be combined with high data reliability and all the advantages of electronic data management.

• In payments, smartphones do not necessarily mean getting rid of plastic credit cards, as shown by the Square service recently launched in the USA. Thanks to a card reader that plugs into smartphones and tablets, credit cards can be accepted anywhere, which can be very useful for proximity services, from the plumber at the end of their visit to taxi drivers, etc.

New acceleration

If 2009 witnessed an explosion of mobile commerce, 2011 will see the exponential use of mobile transactions in our day-to-day lives, thanks to the conjunction of many long-awaited factors (mobile broadband, localisation technology, NFC chips embedded in mobile phones, enhanced terminal ergonomics) and new usages (apps and localised social networks). Such transactions are now widely used for mass-market services, but also by smaller businesses in their service delivery.

What next? In such turmoil it is difficult to predict new mobile services very far ahead. Emerging countries have invented new paradigms to solve specific day-to-day issues, and they will continue to do so. In developed countries, mobile transactions will further unleash the extreme sophistication of a context-aware and real-time relationship between consumers and businesses, and marketing plans will be key in 2011 in demonstrating that such transactions convey a real benefit to users.

What we know for sure is that companies should concentrate on mobile transactions that simplify users' lives, as the emerging countries have taught us. For complex transactions such as payments, for instance, the key point will be to have the important players (telco operators, payment associations and services, internet or software giants, phone or computer manufacturers) advance at the same pace and agree on respective positioning and roles in the ecosystem.

Finally, we urgently need to realise that the mobile phone is becoming the backbone of a modern and multi-channel customer-to-business relationship, and companies need to transform their organisations and processes quickly in order to win in this new situation.

Stop selling products, sell solutions

AS THE ECONOMY BECOMES DIGITISED, MANY PRODUCTS HAVE BEEN DEMATERIALISED; THEY ARE NO LONGER WORTH MORE THAN THE VALUE OF HOW WE USE THEM. HERE ARE SOME EXAMPLES AND EXPLANATIONS.

Digital: What are we talking about?

"Digital" entered the enterprise around 15 years ago. Before the emergence of the web, information technology applications were largely deployed to manage structured data. But those applications were only available to employees within the enterprise, or at least integrated with their equivalent by commercial or strategic partners. Digital introduced a new era that emphasises unstructured information and free structured data from large enterprise applications (ERP, CRM and mainframe) through web services. Beyond that, a new set of devices were deployed, deriving from the personal sector and leading to new professional applications.

Peugeot doesn't lease vehicles, it sells "mobility credit". With its new offering known as Mu, UK subscribers are given the chance to rent a choice of mobility solutions ranging from bikes to light commercial vehicles such as scooters in addition to accessories (like trailers and roof boxes) that a consumer needs only occasionally. Peugeot plans to make Mu available in 200 large European cities by 2012, with the aim that UK users will be able to book vehicles abroad using their Mu cards. Mu is not only a clever way of developing the Peugeot catalogue, extending customer relationships and bringing new clients into the Peugeot network, but is also an offering that fosters use over and above the product.

The business market opened up the way

The Peugeot example demonstrates that an underground movement is spreading: our developed societies are gradually moving from an economy of product ownership to an economy of usage. This movement began in the world of B2B and is now reaching the general public. Businesses – often for economic reasons – have long been consuming products in the form of services. Since the 1980s the American firm Xerox has been providing and maintaining copiers for its large accounts worldwide, and charging by the copy. Veolia Environmental Services sells degrees of comfort to a municipal swimming pool rather than kilowatt-hours. In the laundry business, Elis supplies and washes laundry for professional use at a flat rate. This change is affecting IT as well. The market for the SaaS model (Software as a Service), billed monthly by the number of users, is growing three times as fast as software bought under licence.

Four forces at work

There are at least four reasons why products are now being eclipsed by their content. The first is the dematerialisation of a number of media forms, which in itself is a manifestation of the digitisation of the economy. It is happening in news and entertainment (press, music, books, films, software, etc.) where physical media are gradually giving way to their digital equivalents. There's even an online version of *Monopoly* – traditionally a board game! The move towards sale by usage (or "pay-as-you-go") is a natural one; because marginal production costs tend to be close to zero, the selling price of the product is no longer an issue. The only value lies in the access to and use of the content. Spotify, the online music streaming service, had approximately seven million users globally as of early 2010; about 250,000 of these are paying members. Spotify is funded by paid subscriptions; charging £9.99 per month for a premium subscription. In these economic models the price of the physical platforms tends to be included in the billing by use, or in the case of Spotify, by a monthly subscription. This is the logic behind today's internet boxes and mobile phones. In the future, Apple's iPad might be subsidised by the content accessed on it.

The second reason for the appearance of usage-oriented models is economics. Falling purchasing power is reducing customers' ability to buy, especially consumer goods that have been manufactured for long-term use. Pay-as-you-go spreads the cost over time and can seem an attractive solution for consumers. The third reason is the constant advancement of technology, as innovation reduces product lifespan and forces consumers to buy goods that will be obsolete before they wear out. A textbook case is provided by video players, which have seen several revolutions in less than 20 years: from VHS to digital cassette, DVD, Blu-ray, and soon to come 3D.

The fourth reason is that this race has finally come up against the challenge of sustainable development, which requires businesses to look after their products from design to recycle. Some have seen this as an opportunity to keep in contact with their customers after the transaction.

Managing the product life cycle alongside the use cycle

This new approach to marketing products or content (whatever the right term is now) requires businesses to have a holistic view of their usage cycle, which may not always be the case. This is quite a radical change at all levels, as Figure 9.1 shows.

OLD MODEL: SELLING PRODUCTS	NEW MODEL: SELLING USE
• Objective: produce a lot • Occasional relationship with customer • Innovation to reduce product life and encourage repeat sales • Increase level of equipment	• Objective: foster use • Lasting relationship with customer • Innovation to lengthen product life and limit maintenance • Optimise rate of use

Figure 9.1 Consequences for businesses of moving from the sale of products to sale by use (source BearingPoint)

To change models, businesses must acquire new capabilities in several areas, such as innovation management (making products sustainable), marketing model development (billing per usage rather than per one-off purchase), end-of-life product management (withdrawal from the market, re-conditioning, disposal) and finally analysis of profitability (where usage rate becomes the basic criterion, see Figure 9.2).

Talking up the consumer benefits

The way in which these products are communicated is also impacted. The benefits for the consumer have to be emphasised more than the product specifications. Relationships with customers are evolving. Customers now need service on the ground, including assistance and repairs, to ensure that they get the best use out of the product.

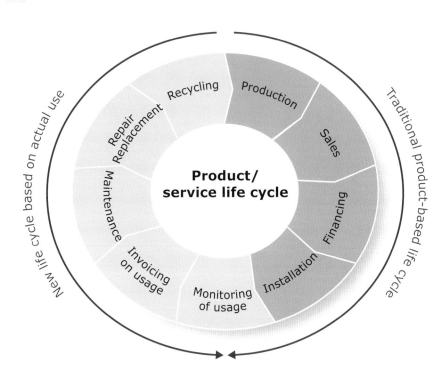

Figure 9.2 Product/service life cycle (source BearingPoint)

There are still hurdles to overcome

While the economy of pay-as-you-go is gaining ground, it is still meeting cultural resistance. The most obvious barrier is the concept of ownership. For many of us owning something brings with it social status, and we still find that hard to give up. In some cases, the attachment to ownership is linked to a miscalculation. We choose to buy something rather than lease it because we have underestimated the total cost of ownership (purchase, maintenance, wear and tear, etc.). The car is a perfect example of this. Think about it – it would be cheaper to rent a car and pay only when you use it, rather than doing what we do and buying one, just to leave it parked outside 90% of the time.

The solution might take the form of schemes such as those offered by StreetCar, a self-service, pay-as-you-go car and van hiring business in England and Scotland. An annual membership costs £59.50, and add-ons including insurance, adding a partner for driving your StreetCar and "anywhere drop-off spots" require a further fee. Subscribers know that they will always find a vehicle available, paying a monthly subscription plus an amount related to use.

This is a step in the right direction. But the revolution really begins when individuals switch most of their consumption to a by-use basis. Could it be that one day we pay for flat-screen TV sets by use, as we already do for decoders and other boxes?

Convince your customers to go ahead... and buy

TO BUY OR NOT TO BUY? THAT IS THE QUESTION CUSTOMERS ARE ASKING THEMSELVES. AT A TIME WHEN PURCHASING POWER IS UNDER PRESSURE, ANY OBSTACLE TO DECISION MAKING BECOMES AN EXCUSE TO DELAY OR — WORSE — ABANDON A PURCHASE!

Consumer indecision can be countered in three simple steps: guide, simplify and reassure. According to various studies, 60-75% of online baskets are abandoned at checkout. But this does not include consumers who did not even dare to create a basket because of the difficulties they experienced. We could guess that most online purchases are not completed due to technical problems, although according to the same studies this is true in only 21% of cases. There are clearly other reasons why consumers are abandoning their purchases.

The internet is not the only place where sales are not completed. Every day in shops, customers experience obstacles to making buying decisions that are mostly due to attributes of the product (see Figure 10.1). The first is information. Either there is not enough, and customers don't have what they need to select the most suitable product available, or there's too much and they are overwhelmed. Alternatively the information may be available in the right quantity, but written in a way demanding that the customer has to be an expert to understand it. This is typically the case when buying a technology product (computers, mobile devices, etc.). Another obstacle is fear of risk, where consumers hesitate as they are torn between the urge to splurge and being more frugal. The reluctance of a chief breadwinner to make a financial investment is understandable, especially in the current financial climate.

Figure 10.1 The six possible obstacles to a buying decision (source BearingPoint)

The final obstacle is that of fear of the unknown. Customers have to make a decision they have never made before and might never make again, without any point of reference. An example of this could be the purchase of a second home or choosing a heart specialist, two situations that do not arise every day. Whatever the nature of the obstacle, the result is the same. Customers don't know what decision to make, and then anything can happen: the purchase can be postponed or, worse, cancelled.

Clearing the path to a decision

Consumers look for reference points to help them make decisions. Brand is a powerful reference point, habit is another. People also tend to buy
Guide, simplify, reassure
the same product because they are familiar with it, even if it is unsatisfactory; or to copy others, as in the example of a consumer who is not a wine buff and who buys the best-selling bottle to reduce the risk of purchasing a low-quality wine.

To guide consumers to more sales, businesses can exploit consumers' gregarious instincts. When internet shoppers buy a book or a CD from Amazon's online shopping website they are informed that customers who bought the same product also liked certain other books or CDs. Guiding customers in the right direction may seem obvious, but the path that you want them to follow must be as clear and simple as possible! SuperQuinn, one of Ireland's largest supermarkets, has placed a sticker on products to assist customers in identifying the lowest-priced product in a particular category, and Yo Sushi, the Japanese sushi restaurant franchise, allows diners to make decisions based on colour-coded dishes (priced between £1.70 and £5) at a glance, thus guiding and simplifying customer choice. Similarly, the Japanese shop chain ranKing ranQueen has adopted a radical approach. On the shelves of each section only the current three to five best-selling toothpastes, chocolates, mobile devices etc. from other stores are displayed, based on independent studies. This is a surprising strategy at a time when other distributors are trying to differentiate their product range! Another example of guiding consumers is on the Fnac website in France, where online shoppers are able to choose products using ordinary language rather than on the basis of incomprehensible technical specifications. For instance, they can check "I want a camera for taking pictures of far-away subjects", rather than having to ask for a camera with 70-200mm zoom lens.

After guidance and simplification, we need to reassure, which removes the final obstacle to buying by allowing customers to make mistakes. IKEA is a good example of reassurance, allowing customers to test its mattresses and to bring them back and choose another within 90 days if they are not satisfied. IKEA's "90 Day Love It or Exchange It" campaign in the UK and Ireland implied that the company recognised the importance of its shoppers choosing the right mattress for support and comfort to suit individual needs. This personalised the brand further and developed brand loyalty. In addition, the initiative aimed to drive away the misconception that low price, which IKEA is known for, equals low quality as well as to highlight the rigorous testing undertaken across the mattress range.

Charging on a pay-as-you-go basis

These three stages will go some way towards reducing customers' indecision, but the price of a product or service is still a major obstacle. Distributors have a real opportunity to lower the initial price obstacle by devising alternative sales mechanisms. For instance, there are two-stage systems where appliances are sold at a low initial price and then subsidised by the regular sale of accessories or services. Electric razors, espresso machines and mobile phones are sold using this model. This original method of charging for use rather than ownership could be a differentiator in the market. Michelin sells tyres to road hauliers by the kilometre so that they don't have to worry about maintenance or replacement. Could this type of thinking be extended to washing machines, which could be maintained by the distributor and charged by the number of loads washed?

Help for online buying at the point of sale

Obstacles at the point of sale could be removed in a similar way to "cookies" which recognise consumers online and record their preferences. In this way, a loyalty card would not only identify you but also allow you to order your favourite meal in a fast-food restaurant. Something else adopted by online shopping websites that could be used in the physical shoppingworld are customer ratings, where product labels could display a star rating to share other customers' opinions of the product. This approach to transferring good practice is another way in which the two worlds could be brought a little closer together.

11

Make your customer contact points both relevant and economical

AS CHANNELS HAVE PROLIFERATED OVER TIME,
THEIR PURPOSES HAVE OFTEN BECOME CONFUSED.

The current economic crisis provides an ideal context for reviewing customer contact channels. Is the world of customer relations at risk of falling into anarchy? In particular, with the expansion of the internet, managing multi-channel communication has become even more complex. Today, points of contact (shops, internet, call centres) all tend to share the functions of customer relations, but these expansions have not always been properly thought out.

In shops, which are still the main places for transactions (indeed the only place where customers take away the product they have bought), logistics (after-sales service) and relationships are also given an "experiential" role. They are reconfigured as play areas or temples, where customers can have a memorable (and sensory) experience with the brand. It is known as "retailtainment". A telco concept store for instance, includes a sales area, restaurant, bar, concert hall and musical showers! The sustained rate of bank branches opened in the past few years and the explosion of showrooms (Nespresso, Orange, Toyota) are other examples of this. At the other end of the chain of points of contact, call centres that handle customer relations continue to carry out transactional functions. Finally the internet, which traditionally has a role in information and transactions, is increasingly handling customer relations following the explosion of Web 2.0. Online, the influence of consumer communities is palpable. Business is seeing a whole section of customer relations shifting towards these forums. Just launch one dodgy product and a whole community will be talking about it in an instant!

Dictated by economic efficiency and customer demand

The transfer of the functions of a channel of interaction (transactional, relational, logistical or experiential) from one point of contact to another is an almost natural shift (see Figure 11.1). But the transfer phase goes hand in hand with confusion that is costing business dearly, and who can afford that any more? The recent crisis is an opportunity to rethink customer relations, based on a rupture model and from the viewpoint of operational efficiency. This can only be done by redistributing the functions of the various points of contact. This movement is already taking place. Some businesses – principally in the banking sector – are encouraging their customers to carry out simple transactions, historically carried out by call centres, on automated channels (web and interactive voice response systems). Telephone support staff can then concentrate on complex or high value-added operations, thereby reducing the number of calls and hence the cost of customer services. Others such as Microsoft have opted to back the transfer of the relational function towards the web and its surfer communities. A URL link on the site of the world's top software company redirects surfers, for certain issues, to the Microsoft Communities portal. Shops, however, will remain the only way of

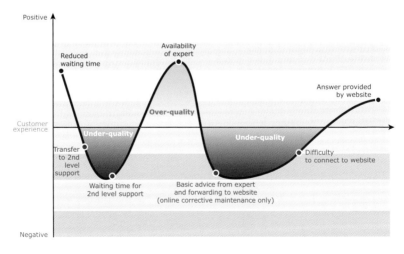

Figure 11.1 An almost natural shift (source BearingPoint)

providing the emotional part of the customer experience, sometimes taking it to the extreme. In the 25 Nokia Experience Centres there is nothing for sale! And for a good reason; the sole purpose of these mutant points of sale is to enable Nokia mobile phone owners to discover new uses, and for prospective customers to take part in product demonstrations.

It is not only economic logic that is pressing for a redefinition of channel allocations. Consumers are demanding it too. They are both more mature and more demanding, and are increasingly able to assess whether the information they are given is coherent, accurate and useful. This explains their desire to deal with the channels suited to their needs and also businesses' obligation to communicate clearly the role of each of its points of contact.

Persuading and dissuading

While the direction to be followed is clear, we still need to find a way of directing customers towards the appropriate channel. The first lever, and one of the most effective, is by charging. This effectively implements a type of "positive discrimination" in favour of one channel. Air France offers travellers the opportunity to buy tickets online at no extra charge to encourage them to carry out the transaction on its website, while the same service costs €5 if they choose to purchase via the call centre. Advertising and communication in general are also designed to attract customers in the chosen direction. Advertising by mobile telephone operator SFR over the Christmas holidays told its customers that they could collect their present from SFR shops, its sales network.

Finally, when persuasion is not enough, businesses can always remove the choice! This is the approach of easyJet and ID TGV for selling their tickets. They sell their tickets on the internet only. This decision has enabled the French railway operator and the low-cost airline to drastically cut their marketing costs.

Pushing the logic a notch further

Since economic efficiency and customer demand are pressing for a clear allocation of functions between the channels, why not take advantage of this to follow the logic one step further and face up to some embarrassing questions. For example, "Do I still need my chain of shops?". The florists Aquarelle used to have some 20 shops and decided to close most of them, keeping only a few and focusing on e-commerce. Another question relates to mail-order houses whose economic model is in crisis leading to big cuts (see Figure 11.2). Without going so far as to remove access to a contact channel, the most effective persuasion policies today are those that offer a richer customer experience. To cut waiting times at its counters, Air France is encouraging passengers to use online

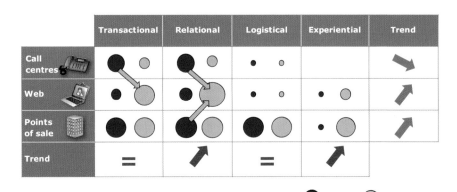

	Transactional	Relational	Logistical	Experiential	Trend
Call centres	● ○	● ○	• ○		↘
Web	● ○	● ○	• ○	• ○	↗
Points of sale	● ○	● ○	● ○	• ○	↗
Trend	=	↗	=	↗	

● Today   ○ Tomorrow

Figure 11.2 The new balances in customer relations (source Bearingpoint)

check-in, and to persuade them to change channel it is allowing them to choose their seats 24 hours before flying and print out their boarding cards. After a period of adaptation, the customer is satisfied with the service and the business has done well out of it. A customer relations strategy that makes perfect sense in a time of crisis and looks set to last.

Simplify for success

COMPANIES ARE SUFFOCATING THEMSELVES WITH
OVERLY COMPLEX COMMERCIAL OFFERS AND
CUSTOMER CONTACT PROCESSES. THEY BORE THEIR
CUSTOMERS, WEAR OUT THEIR EMPLOYEES AND
WEIGH THEMSELVES DOWN WITH UNNECESSARY
ADMINISTRATION. IT IS NEVER TOO LATE TO SIMPLIFY.

Imagine this scene in a customer relationship department: a customer calls her supplier because she has seen an advertisement and wishes to switch to the brand new subscription offer – the more sophisticated and hence more expensive option. At the other end of the line, the agent should promote this sale, encouraging the customer's aspirations to purchase this top-of-the-range subscription, which will in theory get him a commission. Yet, he does all that is possible to postpone the sale! Why? Simply because recording the new subscription requires complex, manual processes and he knows from experience it will be the source of endless problems with the invoicing department or with others internally.

Even though this example is hypothetical, the sentiment is not exaggerated. In fact, it is very similar to reality and unfortunately happens every day. But are companies to blame? Caught between technology innovation, increasing customer expectations and the rise of "low-cost" providers, they feel forced to multiply launches of new products and services with the result that customer relationship management becomes more complex. Although there is frequent talk of refining the targeting of special offers in order to make them more relevant to different customer segments, companies are also driven by the need to be in the news, taking up space on consumers' overloaded memory disks.

Cost of complexity

Amid the jungle of commercial proposals and business cases, the proliferation of offers in companies' catalogues end up creating a complex world in which it is difficult to detect a company's priorities. The eagerness to launch new products is often pursued to the detriment of upstream preparation (tests, logistics, customer service), which sometimes reaps disastrous results (product recall, unavailable stocks, overwhelmed after-sales services, etc.).

Historically, dissatisfied customers remained scattered with no real means of coordination and the brand image did not suffer too much from such problems. But with forums and blogs, things have changed. Dissatisfaction makes more noise. Consumers are lost and irritated by excess information and companies' inability to manage the complexity of products they place on the market. And they let companies know. As an example, almost a quarter of inbound customer contact in the telecom and media sector is related to invoice queries prompted by the fact that customers cannot see the link between their invoice and the service they have subscribed to! The profusion and complexity of offers has even more unexpected consequences. It demotivates employees who fluctuate between hopelessness and confusion, as we have seen in the example at the beginning of this chapter. Indeed, although head offices are obsessed with accelerating speed to market, they do not always take the trouble to ensure that priority and

Offering rationalisation and simplification benefits sales and service

time is given to training call centre agents.

Management must better coordinate innovation efforts between upstream marketing and customer service. This will enable them to market new offers while guaranteeing after-sales service quality. Financial cost also remains a key consideration. The amount required to expand the product and service catalogue must also be taken into account. The profusion of offers leads to an increase in administrative charges as each addition further overloads the operations and management teams. These incremental costs are hardly ever recorded in the books. Conversely, the simplification of product and special offers structures has positive downstream effects on marketing and after-sales services: distribution channel and call centre operators are trained more rapidly and more systematically, the dialogue is easier, the management more fluid… and the customer more satisfied.

Hiding complexity and presenting simplicity

Simplification: Bouygues Télécom has achieved this with its invoicing process. Rather than send its customers an email, which may get lost in their inbox full of spam emails, the phone operator warns them each month, by text message, that their payment has been credited to their account. This is a fast, economical and easy acknowledgement of receipt. Some companies have understood the benefits they can gain from the simplification of their contact procedures. They introduce indicators on their dashboard that measure customers' simplicity perception. Internal as well as external surveys provide feedback on each step of the customer cycle (see Figure 12.1).

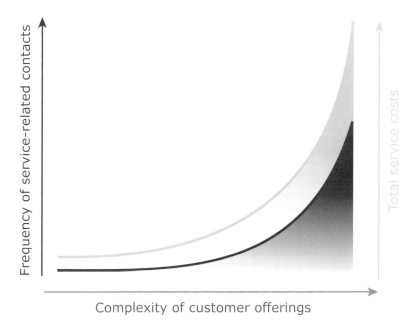

Figure 12.1 Variation in service costs and contacts depending on customer offerings (source BearingPoint)

However, simply monitoring the level of complexity is not enough; product rationalisation with simplified offerings is what will make the difference. Dematerialisation enabled by the shift to digital processes is a precious ally to support this process. As an example, ticketmaster.com has made a specialty of it. It dematerialises tickets for cultural and sports events: customers who buy their tickets on the internet can print or receive a bar code by text message. It will be scanned at the show's entrance, and will act as an entry pass. But one of the most accomplished examples of simplicity is exemplified by Google. Despite the complexity of algorithms that are run behind the scenes and the billions of terabytes of data to which its engine gives access, its front page is characterised by extreme simplicity. This simplicity is what web users acclaim, and probably explains why 80% of US internet users visit Google daily.

Reduce over-quality

EXCESS QUALITY IS A LUXURY THAT BUSINESSES CAN NO LONGER
AFFORD. THEY NEED TO REVIEW THEIR QUALITY STANDARDS,
EVEN IF IT MEANS LOWERING THEM IN CERTAIN CASES.

Cutting quality standards can be done without harming a company's sales or image, provided that customers do not notice the changes. For instance, it is absurd for a business to pay the extra cost of 24-hour delivery to customers who are not in a hurry! It would be better to introduce a standard 48-hour delivery and charge extra for a 24-hour service to customers who want it. This is just one example of combating over-quality. Reducing excess costs makes sense in the world of customer service too, even though it was manufacturing industry that paved the way by tracking excess quality in production processes. Using methods such as value analysis, it was possible to take a fresh look at products and adapt them to users' needs while cutting costs.

But before we look at ways of tackling over-quality, we need to define it. It can be understood as delivering a level of quality higher than the customer perceives. In other words, it is a form of wastage of business resources. Contagion between business sectors is largely responsible for this failure. All businesses observe the practices of their neighbours: so bankers examine the world of retail while energy suppliers may take inspiration from the mobile phone market. "Best practice" in a successful sector quickly turns into quality standards that must be applied quickly to others. The examples are well known: "80% of calls must be answered in under 20 seconds"; "a customer must not spend more than 30 seconds on an interactive voice response system"; and "collect as much customer information as possible during a call". These indicators are not relevant in all sectors or for all businesses, and yet people tend to jump on to the bandwagon. Finally, and above all, where are the customers in all this? There's nothing wrong with deriving inspiration from the competition's good ideas, but be careful not to lose sight of customers' needs!

Detecting pockets of over-quality

Rooting out excess service helps make considerable savings. To reveal pockets of over-quality on paper, just compare the real performance of the service, as measured by the indicators, with the efficiency perceived by the customer, as reported in customer satisfaction polls or net promoter scores (NPS). In principle, businesses have all the tools to do this: service quality reporting and customer satisfaction surveys are institutionalised nowadays, while net promoter scores quantifying brand loyalty are gradually being introduced. But the real challenge is to compare these measurements. Indeed, few businesses think of crossing the two parameters – performance of the service and customer satisfaction – as the figures tend to be used only in the departments where they originate. Only a few pioneers have succeeded in correlating them. A mobile phone operator has compared the time customers wait to be connected to a representative with their inclination to recommend the company. It turns out that customers do not penalise the company if they wait a few seconds more, but this short extra delay could allow the company to reduce the number of representatives on hand and eventually save millions of euros. So, no panic. This example demonstrates that level of service can be reduced to an acceptable extent without causing customer dissatisfaction (see Figure 13.1).

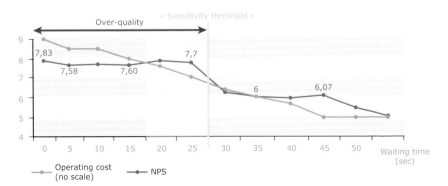

Figure 13.1 The "sensitivity threshold" optimises resources while maintaining an equivalent perception of the quality of the service (source BearingPoint)

This observation opens up new horizons. Now we can systematically seek out areas in which customers do not notice any reduction in quality, up to the point known as the "sensitivity threshold". And there is an almost infinite number of subjects to study. For examples, compare staff training hours with the net promoter score to determine just how much training is needed to ensure full customer satisfaction; or correlate mail handling times with the net promoter score to adjust them to the ideal value. This examination also enables the critical points to be updated at which a person becomes a promoter of the company or conversely joins its detractors. All operations can be put under the microscope (processing time, turnover, "Once and done" processing, etc.), but don't expect them all to reveal pockets of over-quality.

Ways to reduce over-quality

With these reference points in mind, business decision makers are armed to tackle the over-quality issue. Several solutions are available, such as encouraging the use of automated contact channels or forums on the internet, discouraging access to contact centres for certain issues, charging for services that were previously free, or even abolishing certain services (see Figure 13.2).

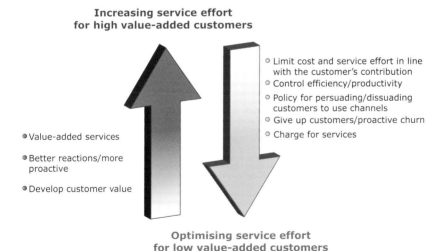

**Increasing service effort
for high value-added customers**

○ Limit cost and service effort in line
with the customer's contribution
○ Control efficiency/productivity
○ Policy for persuading/dissuading
customers to use channels
○ Give up customers/proactive churn
○ Charge for services

● Value-added services

● Better reactions/more
proactive

● Develop customer value

**Optimising service effort
for low value-added customers**

Figure 13.2 Do more with less… : differential treatment
(source BearingPoint)

Companies may opt for various strategies. The first and most radical consists in reducing the level of service for all customers, based on the sensitivity thresholds observed beforehand. The disadvantage of this method is that it penalises all customers, including high-value ones. So introducing differentiated treatment can be a more suitable strategy. The business guarantees impeccable service to its core customers; for the other 80% – who often generate only 20% of the results – it matches the level of service to their level of contribution. It is better to ensure that high-value customers receive high-level services rather than providing everyone with an average service.

Finally, why not adopt another strategy that could give customers the choice? According to their day-to-day needs, customers would be free to choose between over-quality or low-cost services. This has indeed been well understood by some companies. For instance, taxi companies offer their customers priority care if they pay an extra charge. Similarly, easyJet's "speedy boarding" service provides passengers with a dedicated check-in area and priority boarding so that they can choose their seats, and only for a few euros more. The only limit is your imagination...

Use payment experiences to drive competitive advantage

THE WORLD OF PAYMENT IS UNDERGOING A
REVOLUTION; TRADITIONAL METHODS ARE
IN DECLINE AS NEW ONES APPEAR. THESE
CHANGES HAVE A PURPOSE: TO RATIONALISE
AND STREAMLINE CHECKOUT FOR THE BENEFIT
OF BUSINESSES AND CUSTOMERS ALIKE.

Is cash on the way out? It is expected that by 2014 coins and banknotes will no longer be used in Dutch supermarkets, and will be completely phased out in the country by 2015 (source Consumentenbond, the Dutch consumers' association). Cash costs money. A recent study published by Retail Banking Research claims that the use of banknotes and coins costs each European citizen €130 a year. And this does not include cheques, which have already disappeared in the Netherlands and are on the way out in Belgium, Germany, Switzerland and Sweden. They are still in widespread use in the United States and France, but have been on the decline since 1990 in the UK where only 3% of payments (worth just 2% of retail turnover) are made by cheque. It is planned to phase out cheques completely in the UK by 31 October 2018, after some 350 years of loyal service.

world to mobile phone operators. This is a huge challenge. If you consider that the mobile phone is an almost universal item (there are about four billion of them in circulation in the world), the cashless society is more likely to come about using mobile devices than it is with credit cards. If the mobile phone is to become the new wallet for all of humanity, then all the players involved (telephone manufacturers, mobile operators, banks, technology suppliers) will have to agree on a single standard platform capable of handling calls, payments and even loyalty schemes.

A tougher change for small traders

In the end, the choice of payment method could become as much of a competitive element for retailers as product and service offerings. Ease of use is becoming increasingly important in the eyes of consumers, and so the greater the variety of payment methods offered to customers, the more likely it is that a customer's loyalty will be secured. But as nothing is ever simple, retailers must also ensure that the transaction does not become overcomplicated. Lastly, traders have to find a way of accommodating customers who want to self-checkout as well as those who want to be served at the checkout.

No matter what, retailers will have to promote both cashless and contactless payment systems. The major chains will be able to turn this corner with relative ease, but the playing field is not level for all players. Small independent traders are likely to face complications as introducing contactless payment technology might be prohibitively expensive as in the ongoing assessment at Tesco's. Banks and financial services will need to take this into account. A revolution cannot succeed without a struggle.

15

Use electronic billing as a springboard for your digital customer relationship

CUTTING DOWN ON PAPER BILLS IS NOT JUST
ABOUT CUTTING COSTS. IT'S ALSO A LITTLE-
USED MEANS OF ESTABLISHING A CONSOLIDATED
DIGITAL RELATIONSHIP WITH YOUR CUSTOMERS.
HERE WE PROVIDE A PRACTICAL GUIDE.

Businesses have discovered that 20-30% of their most profitable customers choose the internet as their preferred contact channel. Logically, these are also the customers who are most willing to view their bill in their own time in the evening or at weekends.

With good things coming in pairs, a recent study by an American telephone operator revealed that people who sign up for electronic billing are among the most loyal (+15% retention) and the most profitable (+20% of margin) (Forrester report, March 2009). This is a significant finding: a customer who chooses electronic billing is prepared to accept the internet as a contact channel, and is taking a first step towards a digital relationship with their supplier. Businesses today are missing a great opportunity by not capitalising on these new behaviours.

A tool for creating traffic

Just emailing a PDF invoice identical to the paper original to your customers is not enough to engage in a digital relationship. Nowadays customers expect more. They expect to see their invoices in a dedicated space, and online customer spaces are the first step towards building a lasting dematerialised relationship. These private environments can be customised to offer greater content and services adapted to customers' profiles. Businesses continue to compete with one another for innovative ways to entice their customers into visiting and using these spaces (see Figure 15.1).

Vodafone Live! is an entertainment, music, sport and information portal that can be accessed from any WAP-enabled mobile phone. Similarly to Google, Vodafone Live! tracks customer downloads and suggests new products based on their behaviours.

The portal of a telecom operator can mimic Google and change its look based on a customer's preferences, enabling surfers to build their own customised space. When offered good tools, customers are much more likely to provide their email address, for example. But this is not the only attraction – each billing service that

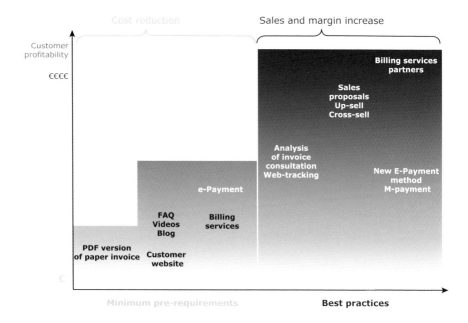

Figure 15.1 Leveraging electronic billing
(source BearingPoint)

these portals are able to manage (payment, lodging complaints, aftersales service) means fewer demands on customer service.

Revealing the customer profile

Each time customers check their electronic invoice through their dedicated space they give businesses a brilliant opportunity to capture their browsing habits through "web tracking" and so get to know their customers better. For example, whether or not the user opens the invoice is information that should be interpreted. Opening it could mean either that subscribers don't entirely trust their supplier or that they want to control their consumption: the business can work out which of these interpretations is correct by relating the information to the type of customer.

Electronic billing can reveal information to help you know your customers better

Similarly, detecting a customer who very rarely looks at invoices and then starts to open them every month can be used as an alert for customers who maybe feel they are paying too much.

It's obvious how businesses can benefit from this information. It may sound surprising, but electronic billing plays a large part in customer relationship management through the lessons that can be learned from it and it can also contribute more generally to customer orientation policy, calculating scores and segmentation.

Those who prefer an electronic versus a paper invoice are almost always the business's best customers. This is confirmed by a study conducted by an American online bank that found a correlation between consultation of electronic invoices and customers' average spend. The more they consult and pay their invoices on line, the higher their average basket (Forrester report, March 2008). The study also suggests communication campaigns to take better advantage of all the levers offered by electronic billing. One of these is through emailing the latest bill to customers, and inviting them to click on a link to view it. This is a sure-fire way of generating traffic to the customer web space.

Each visit to the site is an opportunity to expose customers to offers without harassing them, leaving the next step up to the customer, and seeming much less intrusive than a conventional marketing campaign. If a business wants to generate traffic to its website, online bill viewing is not the only way to achieve this. Customers who do not wish to pay by direct debit could be invited to pay by bank card or bank transfer directly on the website.

Keeping tabs on electronic billing

This can also give access to new modes of payment developed by third parties such as PayPal, or encourage customers to use m-payment. Offering innovative services around electronic billing means businesses can transform a rather difficult but necessary stage in customer relationships (payment) into a simplified customer experience. It is also a way of distinguishing yourself from your competitors.

Remember, it is important not to lose control of your electronic billing! Virtual vaults or safes is a concept under development where an online secure repository exists for individuals to store digital documents, such as their bills, over the long term. Once set up, some virtual safes can automatically fetch bills from their issuer. The development of virtual safes has revealed some risks, but if one day these services are successful then business customer web spaces will be abandoned and a whole host of information about customers will be lost.

Unless businesses create their own safes, they must start to consider partnerships with the promoters of these solutions. The result might be, for instance, creating access to the customer space directly on the safe site, so as to consolidate a dedicated and regular space for communicating with end-users.

Attracting your customers to electronic billing and capitalising on knowledge of customers

Involve your customers in your R&D

INVOLVING CONSUMERS IN NEW PRODUCT DEVELOPMENT AND TESTING
HAS BECOME ALMOST COMMONPLACE. ALTHOUGH THIS CONCEPT
APPEARS VERY PROMISING, IT REQUIRES CAREFUL PREPARATION.

The idea that R&D should take place within the four walls of a laboratory has definitely changed. More recently, any web user can now be a potential inventor for companies.

Through the web, companies can invite the general public to participate in the development of their future products and services. This is called "co-creation" or "co-design" and is a natural extension of the emerging "crowd-sourcing" trend in which companies source tasks originally conducted by employees to groups of people outside the firm on a voluntary basis. The idea is simply a way for companies to subcontract research on new ideas to their customers, and it often suits them very well. Companies have always relied on their devoted admirers for ideas through surveys, focus groups and competitions. Now the internet enables them to take this concept further: getting more detailed information from customers and creating long-lasting relationships.

How to give a new role to the customer in R&D?

The first discussion point concerns the appropriate positioning of customers in the life cycle of product/service innovation. Customers can be requested to give their ideas in advance (ideation) or afterwards when product ideas have already been designed (beta-testing). The second issue relates to the degree of openness of the process – whether customers are free to take part in the dialogue (opt-out) or instead are selected beforehand (opt-in). It is important to target a population that is favourably disposed to the brand, who know it well, and to involve partners and the future players of the programme to recruit the required customers. Thus in several schemes, companies only include their own customers, at least initially. Similarly, Petzl only asks its official distribution network to test new products and give feedback. Voyages-sncf.com also uses its customer database to solicit the most appropriate customers for prospective and premium services.

In Europe, one web user in three contributes to the "participative web"

The success of Linux and Wikipedia has proved that web participation is large and growing. Recently, the American airline, Delta, opened an area on its website to customers so they could give their input and suggestions for service improvements. This type of co-creation on the web could in due course become the norm.

In their book, *Groundswell*[1], Li and Bernoff estimate that 10% of European web users create content on the web and 20% react to this content. In total, almost one web user in three in Europe is actively participating on the web. This type of participation from actual and potential customers is really a dream come true for companies, as information is offered spontaneously by the customer. Companies can leverage this to reduce the lead time for launching new products, better serve their customers' needs, capture innovative ideas, and even test future prototypes for free! Co-creation in addition reduces the risk of launching a product or service that is unlikely to be a huge success. In theory we should see fewer product flops as a result. Better yet, consumers can take responsibility for promoting the product because they helped to create it.

Four roles for the "active" customer in R&D

The customer can become active in product development in four main ways (see Figure 16.1). The first role is the "conversation", based on a community platform with a conversational style. This allows companies that are little known to the public (or whose online image appears negative) to initiate a first dialogue on the web, even though this may involve a certain level of management risk. By proposing a topic for discussion that is unrelated to the company's core business, a dialogue can be initiated with internet surfers – for example, on sustainable development and ethics or changes to daily life, such as transport of the future, tomorrow's technology (Cisco), or even about providing funds to develop new products or services (Pepsi) … but also targeting a population whose loyalty has to be developed, where the aim is to involve customers in the creation of enterprise value (Urbania).

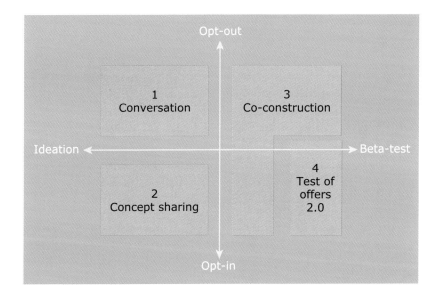

Figure 16.1 Four methodologies for customer collaborative innovation (source BearingPoint Point of View, Innovation 2.0, July 2010)

The second role is "concept sharing" involving an online form on which to submit ideas without being challenged by the community. It is particularly popular with large industrial groups for which R&D represents a significant investment. Then, by allowing customers to submit their own ideas for products, the enterprises intend to complete the internal research efforts by collecting ideas from basic research (Procter & Gamble, 3M Kraft), and new business opportunities that the group may develop in partnership with small businesses or contractors (Unilever, Cisco, BMW, Ben & Jerry's).

Thirdly, "co-construction" is based on creating an online community focusing on improving the relevance of a company's products and services. This facilitates a better understanding of expectations and a stronger customer involvement in the creation of products for the company, allowing customers to give their opinion on products that are under development – e.g. the improvement of product concepts (Dell), the customer experience (Starbucks, Owlient) and advanced testing of a service requiring significant resources (Exalead). SNCF goes even further with its "TGV Lab", which serves as an incubator. It builds real project teams and continues to communicate between internal and external in order to nurture ideas.

Finally, the "test of offers 2.0" role creates an online community to help product managers accelerate innovation market entry. This allows companies to industrialise consumer tests in order to meet the needs of their geographically dispersed population. In soliciting customer "experts" in its products, the company provides a way to validate products pre-launch, using a small target group (the athletes for Petzl, specialists on French search engines for Exalead, "train spotters" for RATP, experts on cashback for Maximiles). Alternatively, it is possible to validate a product by targeting a potentially very large population (Google, Vodafone, Nokia).

Suggestion box or Pandora's box?

Although the examples above illustrate the recent proliferation of co-creation, there are some reservations. First, there is the challenge of processing huge volumes of data in order to extract good ideas. Reading and sorting through ideas takes up human and technical resources. Starbucks cleverly avoided this issue by passing the task back to the web user. Only those ideas voted most popular by customers online were taken forward to be considered for implementation by management.

A second challenge is that of exclusivity. There is no way to ensure that a web user will reserve their idea for one company only, and even if they do, that they won't broadcast their idea to others during the creation process. It is very difficult to work confidentiality contracts into the process of spontaneous web user ideas. Lastly, companies have to consider the issue of payment. If a product becomes a best seller, then its "web inventor" would surely wish to receive a part of the revenue generated by its creation.

A new role: The community manager

The processes discussed here can be brought together by a "community manager", possibly with the support of business ambassadors. Remember also that the selection and processing of ideas may require the establishment of a jury of experts. Cisco's IPrize needs six full-time people during the first two months of each competition. In addition, the company could involve representatives from each of its product lines or services. To some extent the community manager can play a key role for R&D teams, extending their footprint by using open innovation mechanisms to enrich final offer delivery to the market.

Note

1. Li, C. & Bernoff, J. (2008). *Groundswell: Winning in a World Transformed by Social Technologies.* Boston: Harvard Business School Press.

EXPERIENCE
differently
in a digital
world

Fill the gaps in the customer journey

CUSTOMER EXPERIENCE MANAGEMENT IS LIKE
DEMOCRACY: THE CONCEPT TENDS TO SPREAD, BUT
THE APPLICATION TO REALITY VARIES WIDELY.

Starting from a "high-value customer only" buzzword, customer experience is now drawing corporate executive's attention to how well a customer is treated regardless of their status: every customer should be entitled to some sort of experience.

Therefore, companies are beginning to redesign their operations, starting with customer experience end-results in mind. This is a good thing to do, but a few basic rules have to be taken into account:

- **Be consistent.** Because customer experience is more and more cross-channel, companies should focus their attention on delivering a consistent service across touch points and keeping their promise, rather than "delighting" the customer at some point and missing out globally.
- **Establish priorities.** Customer experience is more easily explained than drawn on paper. From the company's point of view, it is a combination of many types of customers experiencing many journeys through many touch points about many products. To start with, one should focus on some journeys and some clients inside the global customer experience.
- **Go into details.** Customer experience failures often result from broken links between otherwise efficient channels. In order to repair them it is first necessary

to track them down and find them, which involves significant effort when the typical process owner tells you, "My process is working fine".

- **Be persistent.** It is one thing to measure customer experience at some point in time, and something else altogether to improve it on a day-to-day basis, despite established corporate silos and shifting business priorities. To do this, companies will have to appoint customer experience representatives.

So why does it not work?

Nowadays most companies, although they largely understand the importance of a consistent customer experience across channels, are doing a poor job at executing. Competition between channels is the rule, due to internal key performance indicators (KPIs) that differ from one channel to another. A recent study showed that, when asked for help about their company's transactional website, 13 call centre agents out of 15 declared they were not able to help and redirected the call (source BearingPoint). This happens when internet sales are allocated to one budget and telephone sales to another.

More often than not, companies present themselves to the market with an internal focus. A corporate website structure, for instance, may replicate a company's organisational chart, and not the way customers want their questions answered. No wonder links between channels are missing: there is rarely such a thing as an official "link" between marketing and sales, or finance.

The importance of consistency

A recent study by *Harvard Business Review* wounded the myth that companies should aim at "delighting" their customers. When 62% of customers interrogated report having to repeatedly contact a company to resolve an issue, keeping the basic promise across channels becomes a priority. A new metric, the "Customer Effort Score", is proposed. This simply measures the amount of effort that the customer must invest in order to enter into a business transaction with a corporation, and first results show that it is even better at predicting customers' future behaviour than the famous Net Promoter Score.

An enjoyable experience is nice, but an average experience is better than an "usus interruptus". Working on customer experience consistency might be less visible than designing new and costly ways to impress your customers, but it is clearer and arguably yields better results.

Focus on a cluster of customer journeys

"Customer experience" is a huge subject area to assess and monitor. To be efficient operationally when it comes to improving customer experience, companies should start with a rather limited ambition, and focus on one product or one group of customers. Once it has run the whole customer experience redesign process, it should then go on to the next product or group of customers. Embracing the whole customer experience concept in a single effort is just too complicated, so focusing initially on the most valuable areas is good practice. And it can lead to surprises: a recent study of high-value customers of a large public company showed that, due to specific processes designed for them, they actually suffered a worse customer experience than other customers: they usually had to go through two circuits – "regular" *and* "high value" – in order to solve just about every problem (see Figure 17.1)!

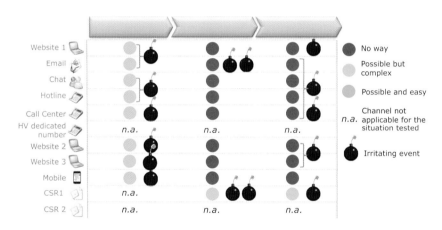

Figure 17.1 Example representation of a customer journey, for one specific product and one type of customer

Detail is key

No one would contest Apple's success in customer experience management. Arguably, Steve Jobs is a visionary who has developed his vision into simple, attractive and cool tools. Others argue, however, that Apple's top management is also obsessed with details, and that is what gives Apple its strength. A customer experience is a lot of details with some high moments. Details should be accounted for, because everybody else in the company already focuses on the high moments.

A review of customer experience by BearingPoint consultants has shown that two-thirds of the annoyance caused by gaps in customer journeys that hinder customer experience can each be resolved in less than one man-day's work: missing link to corporate FAQ, wording changes to give the customer clearer directions, communication on recently opened channels and so on. Customer experience management is not about launching large projects, it is about focused efforts.

France's largest consumer website, voyages-sncf.com, has launched a team whose aim is to spot those small improvements that will make a big difference in customer journeys. Believe it or not, it is called the "Love Team". The Love Team has, since its creation, handled more than 500 improvements, mainly in web journeys, which have been critical in improving service levels.

Develop an internal "customer experience" team

Customer experience management largely exceeds the scope of day-to-day operations. It is quite difficult to monitor using KPIs only, for two reasons. First, very few KPIs measuring cross-channel cooperation and consistency are used in assessing corporate performance. Secondly, customer experience is the combination of channel performance and cross-channel consistency, which makes it even more difficult to measure. Therefore, companies should create an internal operations team with a mission to support and enhance customer experience, and to care about the past, present and future of customer experience. The past is about measuring customer experience results via available KPIs and defining action plans for improvement. The present is hands-on testing of customer experience, from the customer's point of view, and reporting the results. The future is about making sure that the design of new products or services incorporates customer experience focus.

Customer journeys change all the time: new media, products and services create new ways of interacting between a company and its customers, which in turn create gaps between new and existing journeys. Companies put a lot of money into customer interactions: it is the role of customer experience specialists to make sure that this is not thrown into a bottomless pit.

Stimulate your customers' senses at points of sale

SIGHT, HEARING, SMELL, TASTE AND TOUCH: STIMULATE
THE FIVE SENSES TO FIRE UP THE CUSTOMERS'
EMOTIONS AND TRIGGER THE IMPULSE TO BUY. WE
NEED MORE SENSORY MARKETING IN SHOPS.

The five senses are a key to store design. At least one brand has adopted this approach – Lush, the homemade cosmetics company, has a very well-associated brand smell in all its stores. Additionally the store layouts are reminiscent of market stalls with products of different shapes, colours, textures and mood-enhancing perfumes drawing on safe, natural ingredients like fruit. All this attention to detail transforms the prospective customer's visit into a genuine sensory journey, strengthening the brand value/association and awareness. The longstanding major attraction of the Sephora shop found in Paris is its "perfume organ", a circular counter with a sales consultant in the middle who produces everyday fragrances on demand (toast, rubber, hot milk, etc.). Another great example is that of Thomas Pink; the up-market London shirt-maker operates sensors in its global stores that "emit a smell of freshly laundered cotton" as customers walk by.

Enhancing the "customer experience"

By stimulating the senses, the visit to the shop sticks in a customer's memory and the act of purchasing is transformed into an emotional rather than a rational experience. It's all based on a biological phenomenon. Our emotions are orchestrated by codes: light, temperature, perfume and physical contact all stimulate a particular area of the brain. The sensory aspects then stimulate the emotions, which can trigger an impulse buy.

SuperQuinn in Ireland has positioned its bakeries in close proximity to the entrance of all its stores to ensure freshly baked products are the first thing smelt by passers-by, enticing them to enter the store and make a purchase. They have also strategically manned the bakery counters with the most outgoing, "friendly" and best-trained employees, to give customers a more enhanced customer experience. Furthermore, coffee cup-holders have been added to customer trolleys so they can enjoy a fresh brew with their shopping experience.

Some brands pursue sensory marketing to entertain customers and reinforce the customer experience. This way of selling even has a name: "retailtainment" which transforms the customer experience into buying for pleasure. The American supermarket chain Stew Leonard's has taken this to an extreme. Its stores are true theme parks, with characters in costume, living farm animals and, to top it all, a milk bottling plant! The idea is a good one and certainly differentiating, but we should be careful not to ask more of a point of sale than it is designed to do: sell!

In this kind of environment it is obvious that the job description for a salesperson is evolving. They are becoming product demonstrators and store hosts. They are

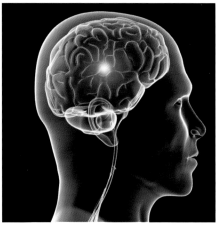

interpreting the signals the customer sends out in order to guide them better, and to fire their imagination by telling them a story around the sensory experience. By way of anecdote, a Chanel salesperson in one of the main London department stores makes no bones about comparing the sound of closing a stick of the brand's lipstick with the dull clunk of... a Ferrari door. Truth is stranger than fiction! The demonstrator is clearly playing on the customer's emotions to close a sale.

Emotional experience 2.0 or the digital customer relationship

This is increasingly easy these days with new technologies that fully support and enhance the effect of sensory marketing. Customers create their own digital experience through natural curiosity. For smell, for example, a new technology can diffuse artificial fragrances in a controlled manner using an alcohol-free and pollution-free vaporising system to prevent the deposit of particles – crucial where food is being prepared. There has also been clear progress in visual renditions by virtual reality systems, for example where changing rooms are becoming futurist machines. You take a shirt from a rack and expect to try it on discreetly over in the shop's changing room, when actually you are taking the whole collection with you! The intelligent changing room offers types of trousers that go with your choice of shirt, without even having to move around, as the mirror shows you wearing them! Even the Selfridges department store in London has an electronic tailoring service for women's jeans called Bodymetrics which scans customers by laser and feeds the measurements into a machine that sews the trousers to fit.

While the sensory approach has long been and still is a lever for differentiating shops as they compete with the internet, this advantage is becoming less marked as the initiatives and innovations arising out of Web 2.0 start to play on the same register. Customers no longer have to go to the opticians to try on a pair of glasses. They can go to the brand's website and upload a photo of themselves to see what they would look like with the glasses on. It's easy: just choose the frames from the online catalogue and slip them onto your photo. And if you need a second opinion, you can even send the picture of your face wearing new glasses to your friends.

The various fields of sensory investment

Everywhere, and in every situation, sensory investment is becoming a priority for surviving increasingly fierce competition. The investment relates as much to shops as to the internet, where a variety of universes can be created. The initiative can be implemented in a variety of fields: new communication technologies sharing sensory information, introducing 3D on websites, recruiting sales staff with facilitation or even acting skills, and training in facilitation, advice and use of products; not forgetting commercial entertainment at points of sale. You do not of course have to do all of this to get started in sensory marketing. Each brand will have to use its own common sense!

Digitise your store

ALTHOUGH E-COMMERCE IS SKY-ROCKETING, STORES REMAIN IN
MANY CASES THE MAIN CHANNEL IN THE CUSTOMER JOURNEY.

I n fact, three-quarters of consumers put the store as their preferred channel.[1]
Nevertheless, the shopper experience is dramatically changing. Digital and
in-store experiences used to be opposed, or at least considered as two different
channels. Companies used to focus on a cross-channel approach to make sure, for
example, that a web consumer would go to the shop – the so-called "web-to-shop"
or "digital-to-shop" journey.

With more than a billion internet devices around the globe, customers are over-
connected and companies have to reinvent the in-store customer experience. Digital
and in-store experiences are becoming more and more mixed, and, put simply, the
shopping experience is moving from "digital-to-shop" to "digital-in-shop".

From "digital-to-shop" to "digital-in-shop"

Over-connected shoppers have taken control of the shopping process. They have
the power to compare pricing (QR code, tag recognition apps), ask for recommendations through social media, double-check product information over the
web, localise a cheapest store in the area thanks to Google maps, make and share
a video of their in-store experience and so on.

Retailers are trying to introduce new devices to attract shoppers and enrich their
experience. These include tablet PCs, touchscreens, 3D, movement detection,

pattern/face recognition, enhanced reality, and tools to localise customers outside the store and offer them specific promotions. Such technologies, which are developing at and around the point of sale, are currently limited and scattered, but these initiatives could lead to new interactions and create new expectations for the customer experience.

According to a September 2010 Gartner study, by the end of 2011 in-store digital marketing will rank as the most important contributor to the success of companies' overall digital marketing strategies. The study goes on to note that, "in-store digital marketing technology, such as smart shelves and digital signage, is 25% more likely to be the choice of marketing leaders over the social web and three times more effective than personal mobile devices."

Companies should be moving from a multi-channel to a cross-channel to a connected customer-centric approach (see Figure 19.1). Customer experience will become the key differentiator of the store channel, while transaction and relation may be supported by other channels. Successful stores will propose an *all-in-one experience* including product demo, pleasure, leisure, community involvement, and all-in-one access to the TV, web and social media.

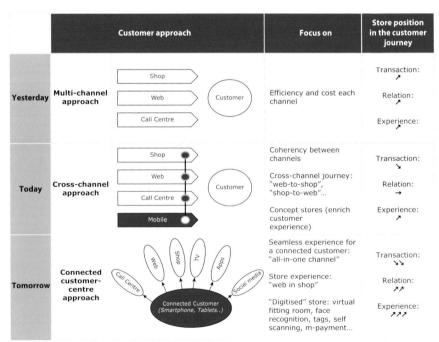

Figure 19.1 Evolution of a channels approach and its impact on the store in the customer journey (source BearingPoint)

The all-in-one experience

Due to the evolution of digital, all channels are now mixed. Retailers will have to go beyond current digital merchandising to investigate new ways to interact with customers and how to enable the all-in-one customer experience. The all-in-one experience means an in-store frictionless experience between the different channels, and mainly requires:

1. Thinking out of the box.
2. Avoiding "dust-trap" technologies.
3. Training and focusing sales reps on customer relations.

Think out of the box: Relation and experience are key

In 2010 the American Umpqua Bank launched what it called the first "neighbourhood store" offering "banking, innovation and a place to connect with the community," said Ray Davis, President and CEO of the bank. "Similar to cafés and other gathering places, Umpqua's neighbourhood stores provide people with an engaging space to browse local merchandise, shop online, enjoy a cup of coffee, and learn about community events and resources – in addition to banking." The interesting part of this example is how the bank continues to invest in technologies and new customer experience: in 2011, it remodelled a part of its stores, adding discover walls, signature services and local spotlights to enrich customer relations and experience (see Figure 19.2).

Each location offers personal banking, mortgage lending, business finance and lending resources in a comfortable, innovative space that features:

- **A discover wall**: These interactive screens digitally showcase neighbourhood events, financial tools, product information and community involvement statistics and opportunities.
- **Return on responsibility**: Customers can learn about volunteer opportunities with local organisations and schools utilising Umpqua's "return on responsibility" module. Return on responsibility features real-time information about community engagement efforts, including hours volunteered by bank associates and charitable contributions made by Umpqua.
- **LocalSpotlight**: This programme features local merchants and their products in-store. To apply, local businesses can visit or call their neighbourhood Umpqua store.
- **A computer café**: Allows consumers to bank online, surf the internet and explore Umpqua's in-store digital experience.
- **Ask me**: A hotline phone that dials the bank's president directly.
- **Umpqua's signature service**: Includes Ritz Carlton-trained associates, and regional touches such as a gourmet chocolate coin with each transaction and videos by Pacific Northwest artists.

Figure 19.2 Umpqua Bank neighbourhood store
(source Umpqua Bank website)

Avoid dust-trap technologies

The number and range of digital ideas and tools aiming at "digitising" stores is booming. For example, for generating traffic, Repetto, the famous fashion shoes brand, has set up an interactive window at its Paris store. Passers-by can modify the scenario of the shop window and make dancers dance on screen through movement recognition. Similarly, Shiseido, the leading Japanese cosmetics brand, has equipped stores (Sephora, Galeries Lafayette, Marionnaud) with a "magic mirror", allowing customers to virtually test make-up on their reflection via enhanced reality. This provides a new selling tool to the sales reps.

Another example is provided by Adidas, which is currently developing "AdiVerse", a virtual footwear wall based on a giant touchscreen and allowing clients to browse and select desired products. Checkout is administered by a sales rep equipped with a tablet PC. This initiative illustrates a completely new in-store customer path. Finally, K, a Belgium mall in Kortrijk, has implemented a virtual fitting room,

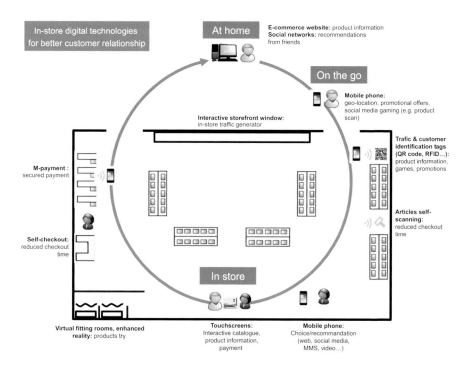

Figure 19.3 Examples of opportunities to digitise the store
(source BearingPoint)

based on 3D modelisation. This allows clients at one location to try the products of all partner shops, with a personal shopper providing guidance on the client's style. These major initiatives (see Figure 19.3) prove that the retail sector is searching out a model for future in-store commerce. Nevertheless, there is a risk to launching multiple initiatives without keeping in mind the basics. As an example, iPad apps or an interactive device not connected to the back office may be useless for sales representatives and may become a dust-trap. To make sure such initiatives are efficient, it is necessary to remember the "3U" concept:

• **Useful:** provide a real service to customers.
• **Usable:** develop a user-friendly interface including simple functionalities.
• **Used:** if the first two "Us" are respected, the service improves its chances of actually being used.

The good news is that retailers have never before had so many technologies with which to innovate. The bad news is that such projects require even more integration than traditional digital projects like websites. Indeed, they bring together two traditionally separate channels: the online and the offline, often managed by different teams in the organisation. Successful projects will also require unusual partnerships between retailers and start-ups or telco operators (e.g. promotions push related to mobile geo-location). Another issue is that sales representatives may be overwhelmed by technology instead of focusing on reinforcing the relationship with shoppers.

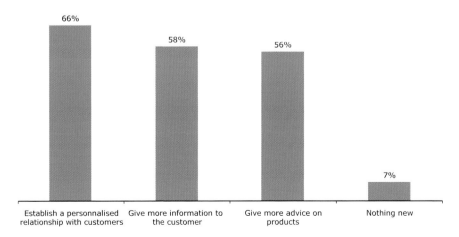

Figure 19.4 What retailers expect from in-store sales reps in an increasingly digital world (source BearingPoint/LSA 2010)

Train and focus sales reps on customer relations

In an increasingly digital environment, retailers expect sales representatives to establish a personalised relationship with customers (see Figure 19.4). To support this new relationship, there must be training focusing on both technology and behaviour. But with the environment and customer maturity moving so fast, retailers will have to regularly rethink their training programmes based on store feedback if they want to enrich the shopping experience.

Note

1. Gartner study, April 2011.

20

Base the virtual community of your customers in the real world

FANS OF A PARTICULAR BRAND ARE NO LONGER SATISFIED
WITH COMMUNICATING JUST ON AN ONLINE FORUM. THEY
WANT MORE. THEY EXPECT TO FIND A REAL PLACE — AN
EXTENSION OF THE WEB EXPERIENCE — THAT ALLOWS
TOTAL IMMERSION IN THE WORLD OF THE BRAND.

According to a 2010 study by Gartner Group, over 60% of the world's 100 top businesses are offering their customers an "online community". Either they have built community spaces around the business's brand or products, such as DestinationSmart.co.uk (Mercedes Benz, Smart Car) or MyStarbucksIdea.com (Starbucks), or they have encouraged or undertaken the building of sites independent of the brand, which offer to exchange experiences between customers (such as ilounge.com). Businesses know that it's worth their while developing or supporting the building of a community site, to separate commercial and relational issues, while establishing a close contact with their customers based on sharing centres of interest, activities and tastes. They also benefit from the site having its own internet address, to avoid it being launched as a Facebook community, which would make them dependent on a third party.

Now that the communities are working, a new issue arises: how to bring them out of the virtual arena? It's obvious in the field of dating; match.com would not have so many subscribers if the men and women who subscribe did not end up meeting face to face! This is also true of other sites such as findyourlocal.com, which extends the concept to a community-based online community built around a pub, where the participants can get to know each other online and meet in person at their local for a pub quiz or to watch a match.

The concept store – a base for communities

We are starting to appreciate that the argument also applies to communities of consumers. The online exchange of impressions is no longer enough: it's rather old hat. We need to go further. The challenge now is to give substance to these groups that for the moment exist only on forums and chats. A comparative loyalty study conducted in late 2008 by BearingPoint in various sectors (telecoms, airlines, consumer credit, retail) confirms this need for grounding in the real world. It also shows the interaction between "off line" and "online" as regards loyalty is tending to become the general rule. Is it sufficient then to decide where to get the members of the community to meet? The physical point of sale is obviously the ideal place, as it is still the place for consumers. The proportion of sales via the internet still accounts for a mere 4% of all retail trade (source Eurostat).

To attract online communities of consumers into the real world and meet their expectations in terms of tangible and multi-sensory experience, businesses must conceive a meeting place that aims to do more than just sell. This new-generation meeting place must also enable consumers to immerse themselves in the world of the brand, its products, technologies and services. The leading consumer electronics companies are already offering a multi-sensory customer experience in the form of the "concept store". The Apple Store on Regent Street in London

even offers a full schedule of training events throughout the day, as well as live music events, competitions and speakers. Just along the street is the Bose flagship store, famous for its *Theatre Show* brilliantly choreographed product demonstration. The demo music is carefully selected and the demonstrators hide and then reveal their small but powerful speakers. This is real showmanship that promises "the ultimate shopping experience" to fans of the brand. In all these cases the goal is the same: to make the "concept store" a place where the customer experience reigns supreme. It's a good start, but it needs to go one step further.

Transforming sales staff into community facilitator

To maintain a community in the physical world, it is not enough on its own to provide a flagship place for the customer experience. Businesses will also have to develop new skills, facilitating and developing community relationships in the real world, while planning to expand them into the virtual domain. Actors will have to ensure continuity by playing the role of go-between for these two worlds. Because they are already in the selling area, sales teams are the natural candidates for this role. Yet they need to be prepared for this change of mission. You can't become a facilitator of physical-virtual communities just by improvising. It's quite a different job, with new objectives and requiring familiarity with new tools. To support staff in this retraining exercise, they will need to be trained not only in facilitation techniques and tools, but also helped to unlearn their conventional sales reflexes. Finally, don't forget to offer incentives in line with their new objectives. Basically, they will have the prospect of enriching their career and opportunities for advancement based on these new skills.

You can get a foretaste of this from the list of Apple Store vacancies: in particular they include the post of "Genius", offering technical support and advice to customers, and "Personal Shopping Specialist" who is to "deliver an unparalleled shopping experience that is truly transformational". Businesses that can succeed in this area will have every chance of meeting tomorrow's community customer relationship challenges.

There have always been physical communities

No need to look far. Clubs, mediaeval guilds or, more recently, professional networks and groups with a shared passion (supporters of sports clubs, fans of artists, etc.). Even in the specific case of consumer groups, there are countless examples of communities forming around a brand and its products. If you need convincing, think of the "chapters", long-standing clans of owners of Harley-Davidson motorcycles such as Planet Biker (the Harley-Davidson community) or the Tupperware demonstration and private sales networks.

of a point of sale. This is a necessary step if we are to invent a new type of customer experience. Some brands have dared to produce a surprise effect by transposing environments. It is interesting to note that not only the luxury brands are recruiting.

For instance, a bank commissioned architect Didier Lefort (the man behind the design for Air France's new first class) to work on its branches using the concept of the "customer as guest". The resulting decor and general ambiance were to make the customer feel privileged and about to enjoy a hotel-style service. The visual result is amazing. The redesigned bank branch looks more like a cosy living room than the reception area of a financial institution!

Apple insists on design even in the after-sales department

While design, as in the previous case, can create a refreshing change between the old and new identities of a point of sale, it also forges a link between a brand's products and its shops. The idea now is to present a coherent profile throughout the customer experience. Products and shops then become harmonious reflections of the brand's position and especially its price image. It would be a mistake to allow any gap to appear between the two, risking customers becoming ill at ease. They would have the impression either that they are not being treated as they deserve – if the products they are buying have a smarter image than the shops – or that they had been mistaken about quality if the products do not match up to their showcase.

The upshot is that design and the customer experience are closely linked. If in doubt, just take a look at Apple. This success story owes as much to the vision of its founder, Steve Jobs, as to its translation into must-have computer equip-

ment, thanks to the work of Jonathan Ive, the company's head of industrial design. Apple products indeed marry unparalleled ease of use with *avant-garde* design, which the markets often then adopt as their aesthetic code. This identity is cleverly reflected in all the customer relations channels: the Apple Stores in the high street and on its website and the after-sales service. Amazing as it may seem, Apple insists on design even in the actions of its after-sales service. If your iPhone breaks down, Apple sends a messenger to pick it up and bring it back after the repair. In addition, the brand transforms each step along this path into many opportunities to measure the unique nature of the Apple experience. The minutest detail counts. In particular, the messenger will use a ceremonial and delicate gesture when taking your iPhone and placing it in a magnificent box, as if it were one of your most treasured possessions that deserved special care. When your iPhone is returned, the ceremony will take place

in reverse. The goal here is to elicit pleasure and emotions that will get you addicted to the brand. Nice work, as it is generally agreed that more than 60% of our purchases are influenced by our emotions.

Artistic directors in industry?

Other companies besides Apple have also institutionalised their use of design. The Australian airline Qantas, which worked on several occasions with Marc Newson and Sébastien Segers in the interior design of its aircraft and lounges, is so convinced of the value of this approach that it has created the post of artistic director for fellow-Australian Marc Newson. This means that design is an integral part of its strategic approach and customer satisfaction. Is Qantas a unique case? Or could we imagine the job of artistic director becoming more commonplace in other service sector or even industrial firms, not only for designing the products but also for conceiving the customer experience? Probably.

But before we get to that point, we could start by involving external designers more in the business's creative process. This can only work if several conditions are met. General management must be prepared for a break with the past, and the operational teams (marketing, customer relations, etc.) must drive design closer to the conception of the business's customer experience. Finally, there must be a thorough and long-term cooperation with the designer to avoid betraying the original intention. In other words, a small cultural revolution is needed.

Make the most of cultural differences in the age of globalisation

IT IS OFTEN DIFFICULT TO IDENTIFY THE CULTURAL
ELEMENTS THAT REALLY DISTINGUISH THE CONSUMERS
OF A FOREIGN COUNTRY. AND WHEN YOU SUCCEED, THE
EFFORTS NEEDED TO ADAPT YOUR OFFERING TO THE
LOCAL MARKET ARE COSTLY. ADVICE FOR SUCCEEDING
IN INTERCULTURAL CUSTOMER MANAGEMENT.

Louis Vuitton bags, Nike tracksuits or Starbucks' cafés, to mention only a few examples, succeed in placing products on the market by giving the impression that they are very similar in nearly every country around the world. Internet trading accentuates the phenomenon. It makes any product accessible to anyone, almost anywhere in the world. Globalisation – because that is what we're talking about – raises a fundamental question about our lifestyles: can the cultural differences between countries continue or will they gradually disappear as standard global consumer habits spread? Businesses would very much like to know the answer, because it is more expensive to adapt customer management by country or region than it is to offer one standard everywhere.

Cultural differences are alive and kicking

Despite globalisation, most products and services will continue to be bought and consumed in each country's own context. Globalisation is not synonymous with standardisation. While consumer behaviour seems to be becoming more uniform from one country to another, it is only an appearance. Countries remain quite distinct; the differences are simply less visible.

As with an iceberg, there is the explicit and visible level of the culture (language, practices, skills, institutions) and the implicit level, which is more hidden (norms, values, etc.). With the effect of globalisation, the explicit elements of culture are becoming more "malleable": products and services, management practice, technological know-how and corporate organisation models are circulating faster and faster in an increasingly open environment. This results in a superficial form of harmonisation of lifestyles and modes of consumption. But at the same time, the implicit elements of culture, the norms and values that represent the core beliefs that individuals and societies have about what is good, right and desirable, are evolving far more slowly. Especially since they have been with us since childhood and are often unconscious. They are the hidden layers of culture, and influence most people's behaviour without their realising.

> *The culture of a people is like an iceberg: you are not aware of its depth simply by looking at it*

One example: nearly two out of three people in the world today have a mobile phone (in a decade, the number of subscriptions has risen from less than 500 million to over 4.5 billion), yet almost universal ownership conceals different consumption habits according to country. For instance, the average monthly talking time varies by a factor of one to three across Europe, and the number of SMS sent varies by a factor of one to five with Japan. Cultures thus at least partially influence average revenue per user (ARPU), even taking account of the effect of differing charging methods in the various markets.

Lessons from the failure of Wal-Mart in Germany

The same applies to the retail sector. Consumers' tastes and behaviours have become one of the main obstacles in the race to expand across borders (see Figure 22.1). Wal-Mart, the world-leading retail giant, entered the German market in 1997 with the aim of shaking up the retail sector through a combination of good service, friendly employees and low prices... and withdrew in 2006. The group failed because it thought it could transpose the formula that made it a success in the United States to the German market. The tightly regulated and very competitive German retail market, where hard discounters (Aldi, Lidl, etc.) account for roughly 40% of groceries sold, proved a major challenge in itself, and Wal-Mart had limited critical mass to start with. However, cultural mistakes also played a significant part in its failure.

Wal-Mart assumed that Germans would like to be treated with the same courtesy as Americans. Staff were therefore taught to greet customers by smiling as brightly as they do in the US and to help pack their shopping. However, according to many surveys, German shoppers hold price and value in much higher esteem than service, and have been accustomed for decades to hunt for bargains without any staff assistance; they would see bag-packing by staff and wonder if they couldn't get their groceries for a few cents cheaper if they packed the bags themselves. As for the institution of the "greeter", shoppers unaware of its key role in Wal-Mart's service concept had repeatedly complained that they had been harassed by strangers on store premises. Consequently, Wal-Mart ended up competing only on price. In doing so, it ran into the strong position of hard discounters in the German market, which ended up being unsustainable (source University of Bremen, 2003).

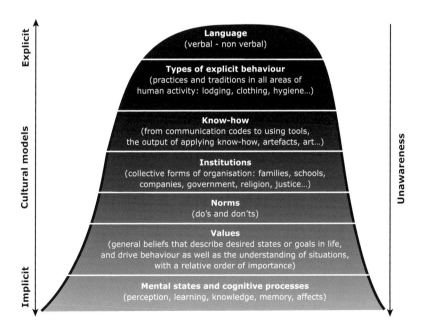

Figure 22.1 The iceberg of cultural levels
(Sources Edward T. Hall, Geert Hofstede, Fons Trompenaars)

The three golden intercultural rules

But beware! Culture is everywhere but doesn't explain everything. Taking national, regional, ethnic or religious platitudes as a basis results in stereotypes that ignore the exceptions. On the contrary, glossing over differences in values and ignoring cultural influences on consumer behaviour is liable to cloud your judgement and any action based on it. Leading businesses have managed to limit this risk by adopting approaches to intercultural customer relations based on values. Their first principle is never to regard their products or ways of thinking and operating as automatically transposable into another culture. In the retail sector, the most perspicacious businesses have widened the aisles of their shops in countries where consumers shop with their families, such as in Brazil. In DIY and other areas, retailers using full-on self-service have evolved towards a sales model offering installation and interior decoration services, especially in China.

A second strategy used to adapt to a local market is to develop services specific to that country, from standard platforms or media. Nokia does this, for example, by studying mobile phone habits in the various countries in which it operates.

 As a result, in India, Nokia Life Tools is a range of local services, available in the various languages of this enormous country where a majority of people still live in villages, which pushes real-time market prices, farming advice and even weather forecasts straight to the mobile phones of its rural customers.

Finally, leading businesses make sure that they use culture as a lever in their innovation and communication. A few years ago, Yum! Brands (KFC, Pizza Hut and Taco Bell) launched an intercultural training and awareness programme for all its managers or franchise-holders throughout the world, aiming to identify the innovations produced by a country or culture, derive best practices for the group from them, and deploy them all over the world, such as the English "breakfast menu" or Krushers and Frutista Freezes fruit drinks (source *Yum Brands 2008 Annual Customer Mania Report*).

In 2002, HSBC launched a global advertising campaign to position its brand using its new slogan "the world's local bank". This campaign, for which HSBC called upon anthropologists all over the world, stresses that you should "never underestimate the importance of local knowledge". The concept was developed following worldwide consumer research which found that, while people appreciate the value of international organisations and services, they question the prevailing "one size fits all" global model. Consumers want to be treated as individuals, and to feel that companies care about them, recognise their needs and understand what makes their community unique. The campaign illustrates this with striking examples of identical objects, numbers, expressions or gestures that mean something entirely different from one country to another. The campaign has been running successfully for several years, and has become a differentiator of the HSBC brand from other financial organisations or global brands.

These examples prove that cultural differences are sometimes subtle and need help to be brought to light. Investing time and effort into understanding these will be required, because businesses that succeed in noting and decoding cultural differences that are significant to consumers in the countries where they operate will gain a decisive advantage over their competitors.

23

Get ready to become a media business

PRODUCING AND MANAGING VISUAL AND AUDIO-VISUAL CONTENT
REQUIRES MEDIA INDUSTRY METHODS, EVEN IN BUSINESSES THAT ARE
NOT MEDIA COMPANIES. LUCKILY, THERE ARE SOLUTIONS. THIS IS A
REVIEW OF SOME PRINCIPLES TO FOLLOW AND THE TOOLS NEEDED.

Trading or media? That is the question for vente-privee.com, the best-known site for selling events in France. Vente Privée, meaning private sale, started out as a European e-trader and is now also a press publisher. *Rosebuzz*, its fashion and culture magazine, is a large, free, bimonthly publication with a print run of 10,000 (they also have a web version) and competes well against the trendiest titles. This e-trader and publisher has even further diversified to become a record label, and has produced a compilation of original tracks, composed to accompany its marketing and sales videos.

Across the Atlantic, Coca-Cola is also thinking about raising its stakes in the media game. The company currently has one of the largest fan bases on Facebook (nearly 23 million) and is apparently considering giving up its official site in the long term to focus on running its Facebook page.

No rich brand experience without creating content

These two examples are evidence of an underlying trend that is directly affecting customer relationships: exchanges between businesses and consumers are gradually moving away from the purely transactional (purchase, delivery, after-sales, etc.)

towards the relational and experiential levels. Experience with a brand is becoming a decisive sales support. This is all the more apparent now that technology has evolved to enable new communication forms between brands and customers (videos on the internet, augmented reality, etc.). All a brand needs to do is to unleash its creativity. For example, transport businesses could decide to promote their premium offerings (First Class, Business Class, etc.) through virtual simulations of the enhanced experience – e.g. they could film short viral videos to effectively demonstrate the added value of the upgraded classes and thereby justify the higher price of these services. The airline Cathay Pacific has recently developed a similar strategy, through demonstrating the various services on board their aircraft via realistic simulation on the website.

Offering digital and media content to customers is no longer a "nice to have" that can differentiate you from the competition, it has become a "must have". However, caution is necessary, as consumers have become accustomed to receiving innovative and up-to-date content from varied industries. To attract their attention, or at the least not disappoint their expectations, a professional approach to content development is crucial. Most major brands have the necessary material to "tell a story" to their customers: origins, know-how, anecdotes, etc. However, the challenge now is to transform these assets, tangible or otherwise, into content that can be exploited via various channels, so as to enhance the experiential dimension of the customer relationship.

Furthermore, while part of the required raw material already exists (advertising, photos, animations, etc.), there is still much to create and especially to adapt to customers' expectations, and also to the constraints of the distribution channels. The solution is that increasingly businesses will have to "think media", and focus on content management and production as a core part of their customer relationships. The most reliable way of achieving this is still to equip yourself with a dedicated strategy, structure and resources, like the mass media do.

New skills and tool

These media-dedicated resources must be invested in acquiring new skills and knowledge, beginning with media management techniques. They will grow in importance as the business's media assets develop (digitisation and indexing of content) and diversify into various forms. Indeed, alongside conventional photos and videos, we are now seeing the appearance of genuine films used as advertising collateral. For instance, Unilever has produced a short movie, called *The Alchemist* starring Catherine Zeta Jones, to endorse its Lux Hair Care product range.

A further point that businesses must consider when developing media is the management of the rights associated with each piece of content. It is a strategic sector, ensuring that the business controls its media assets. There are three factors that merit careful attention with regards to media rights: the duration of owner-ship of the rights to the content and the permission/ability to re-use content multiple times; multi-platform use (internet, mobile, "indoor") so that they can be used in multiple channels; and, finally, the geographical dimension, an essential prerequisite to any international dissemination.

Due to the upstream and downstream use of content, its creation and dissemina-tion also implies extended capabilities for monitoring and measuring audiences. Lastly, as they move into media, businesses will increasingly need to monitor their brand image through tracking and monitoring.

All these above techniques and skills will be fully effective only if they are sup-ported by professional and dedicated resources, as businesses are likely to come up against three recurring issues. The first, is that as content proliferates, they run the risk of losing control of media assets – although this can be mitigated through a solution known as Digital Asset Management (DAM). The DAM concept is embedded in computer tools that provide "intelligent" storage of content, and allows for content to be more readily managed and searched (natural-language searching and indexing), flexible (association of content with tags) and secure. Eventually, this kind of tool will have to become standard and used as the content library for the whole business, for both internal and external audiences (press relations, bloggers, etc.).

The second issue concerns dissemination of content, both with regards to the variety of media channels chosen as well as the rate of dissemination. This issue can be tackled via Content Management System (CMS) tools, traditionally used to manage the publication of content on the internet, but soon such tools will have to embrace the multi-channel dimension. As well as the chosen channels and rate of distribution, the constraints of multimedia dissemination will need to be tackled, and production will have to be adapted to overcome these.

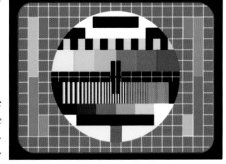

Setting up a media department: The final stage in the evolution

The third and last issue is financial. The more content a business produces, the more budget it requires. However, busi-nesses can limit the extent of these by adjusting the way that they operate. When content is first developed it is mostly left to the specialists (communication agencies, photo studios, etc.), but as needs and volume grow, it can be more economically viable to handle all or part of production in-house (see Figure 23.1). Vente-privee.com succeeded in becoming a real media publisher mainly because the company opted, from its inception, to manage in-house nearly all the production facilities for the content on its site, from photo retouching studios to music production.

Once these challenges have been overcome, businesses have to make one last change: to equip themselves with a proper media organisation. Some have already set up a department for coordinating media initiatives and developing the in-house editorial culture, because they realised that it was no longer viable to merely assist the departments responsible for producing the content (marketing, communication, quality, production, etc.) to build a media strategy. The main role of the new media department is to ensure that the content produced by the business is coherent, whatever form it takes and whatever dissemination channel is used.

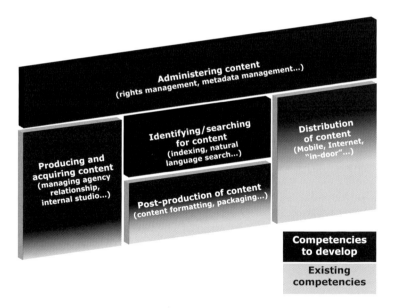

Figure 23.1 Producing, managing and distributing content
(source BearingPoint)

Take the game seriously!

EDUCATIONAL VIDEO GAMES FOR ADULTS – OR "SERIOUS GAMES" – ARE MOVING INTO ALL BUSINESS SECTORS.

Attractive and effective, serious games can quickly train a wide audience in complex subjects. These are valuable training assets in customer relations careers.

Axa, BNP Paribas, Boulanger, L'Oréal, Orange, Renault and Thalys have already trained thousands of their staff, just through play. Smiling on the telephone, welcoming a customer at a counter, making a business recovery, launching a new product – these are some of the skills that these major businesses are developing in their staff using educational video games for adults, known as "serious games". Developed in the 1990s for aviation and defence, serious games are a marriage of video games, e-learning and simulation. Today they are making inroads in all business sectors and functions. Used to facilitate training, learning new skills or for self-assessment, these professional training games are extraordinarily attractive, effective and quick at conveying information and knowledge. In business it is increasingly common for staff to struggle to take in all the messages sent to them, and they often have trouble following the training courses they are offered and acquiring new skills while carrying out their everyday work.

Play is the most effective way of learning

Serious games awaken people's sense of play by combining play with professionalism. They are realistic, interactive and mobile – staff can train themselves on their own PC, iPad or smartphone – they fit the constraints of large corporations and make traditional methods look dated especially the static concept of case studies that training content is still too often based on (see Figure 24.1).

But playing at work, even for training – is it appropriate? If we are to believe Plato, it is. For the Greek philosopher, "the most effective kind of education is that a child should play among lovely things". This applies to adults too! Play actually covers the three main bases in all learning: immersion, which makes the content of the learning more concrete; action, which creates motivation and the desire to discover; and finally simulation, which ensures that the learner's trial and error will not have any unfortunate consequences. Serious games are played in all these registers at once. The serious games' market is expected to grow by 47% between 2010 and 2015, to be worth €10.2 billion by 2015 (although the majority of this growth will be achieved in North America).

These new learning materials also owe part of their success to progress in video gaming and internet technology. Software houses today can simulate any business context and issue in real time and in 3D, using appropriate "gameplay" techniques and the latest video game technologies like augmented reality, or Kinect technology from Microsoft Xbox that enables us to play video games with our own body without additional devices or joysticks.

The Nintendo effect

But technology doesn't explain it all. This educational software is also a hit because a growing number of people – especially, for instance, in France – are into video games. This kind of entertainment is not restricted to young pre-pubescent males or even adults under 25! Some 63.3% of people in France are players, of which 53% are adults and over 52% are women (source GFK study results, 2010). The vast majority of enterprise staff are occasional gamers or even addicts.

Recommended for beefing up training campaigns in business in general, serious games are proving especially effective when applied to customer relations. This is because the customer relations function is becoming increasingly complex as a result of the growth in numbers of products and contact channels. Moreover, businesses focus on customers, and expect constantly improving service and behavioural skills from their staff (hostesses, sales staff, call centre operators, etc.). They usually assimilate these processes and behaviours by repetition. To get the

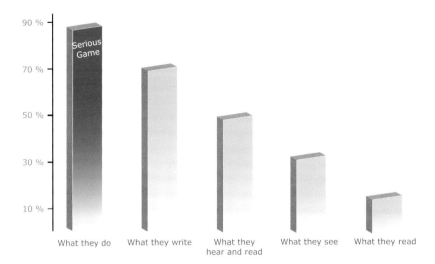

Figure 24.1 What do people remember in a training session
(source BearingPoint)

message across without wearying people, a better solution is by simulating everyday greeting, sales or service scenarios. A final advantage of these games is their
"industrial" power: they can be used to train a large number of staff in a fairly
short time.

For budgets of €50,000 to several million

Be careful, however, not to cast them as magic tools for all needs. The costs of
writing and maintaining these software packages sometimes runs into millions
of euros, and not everyone can afford this. So it's worth developing a game only
if there is a large number of trainees and the training content is complex. For
instance, Pulse!, the most expensive serious game in the world – a hyper-realistic
simulation of an emergency medical service – costs $10 million. If you don't have
that kind of budget, the leading publishers offer generic products that are easily
customised so as to reduce the entry cost, and platforms are evolving to enable
customers to alter their teaching scenarios to suit their needs.

One could have reservations about the development of serious games. By industri-
alising professional practices, is there not a risk of standardising or even schematising
them, thereby stifling creativity and innovation? It's certainly something to watch
out for. But we're not at that point yet. Finally, the use of these professional games

raises other issues. In future, businesses will have to identify good practices so as to incorporate games properly into their training programmes. They will also have to think about organising the time and places to play them. For the time being, there are many different answers depending on the culture of particular businesses – although the recent development of serious games for smartphones provides a clever new way to occupy travelling time (see Figure 24.2)!

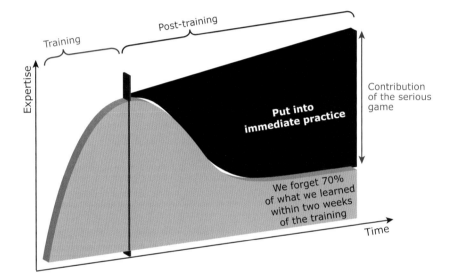

Figure 24.2 The contribution of the serious game: immediate deployment
(source BearingPoint)

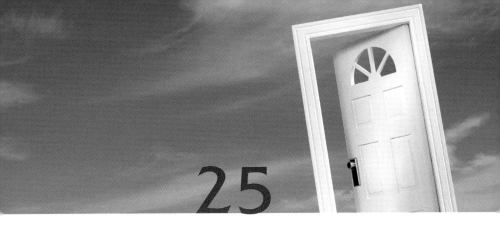

Adapt the internal to the open world

TRANSACTIONS CAN BE AUTOMATED WITHOUT DETERIORATION
OF THE SERVICE LEVEL. RESOURCES CAN BE FREED UP TO
SUPPORT COLLABORATIVE VALUE-ADDED ACTIVITIES.

Companies who decide to participate in collaborative customer relationships will have to make choices. They will not be able to ask their service teams to simultaneously contact consumer communities on the internet for strategic projects, and at the same time run low-value-added transactional operations. Achieving 100% quality across these different interactions is more important than ever before because, thanks to the internet, the general public can publicise its dissatisfaction to a global audience and damage a brand's image in a very short period of time.

Automate the simple tasks

By optimising simple, transaction-based interactions, companies will be able to release resources to manage higher-value-added collaboration projects. Standardising and automating processes involved in basic customer interactions is a good start.

Automation goes beyond incorporating customer interaction areas within corporate websites. It can also be applied to the phone channel through automatic call distribution, and even within sales outlets where electronic self-service terminals can support or maybe replace salespeople. "Subcontracting" the processing of some

customer requests to machines is appropriate. Not only does this strategy enable companies to free up resources but it also reduces workload as well as meeting the customer's need for autonomy. Automation does not necessarily undermine service quality. On the contrary, it can even be a source of satisfaction! To check in for a flight on an electronic terminal, such as those offered by British Airways, guarantees consistent service quality for specific functions: no more misinterpretation of the customer's request or dependence on the receptionist's goodwill. After all, human contact does not always guarantee a better level of service than a machine.

From an organisational point of view, automation will lead employers to redefine their employees' tasks. What new functions can be developed for them to help the journey to collaborative customer relationship management? Ultimately, companies will be forced to reorganise and even to promote customer to customer (C2C) and employee to customer (E2C) relationships through communities. There is every chance that these customer relationship approaches will receive a warm welcome internally. Employees contribute gladly to enhancing directly the dialogue with customers. Numerous examples support this. At online retailer and ticket agent, la Fnac, the team running Fnac Spectacles (the event ticket part of the site) share their own personal recommendations on concerts, artists, exhibitions and plays with web users via a dedicated blog on fnaclive.com. This meeting place does not work just one way: online visitors can also give their opinion.

Companies – a new home for communities

As the appetite for exchanges grows with exchanging, contributors also want to make the most of these new platforms to communicate with each other. This is what we call E2E – or employee to employee – and moves us into the realm of the intranet. A few companies already provide collaborative tools to their employees. These tend to be work-related and are designed to facilitate teamwork across different geographical locations. For instance, BearingPoint uses the web platforms "liveplaces" and "Wiki" to allow consultants who are working on assignments at different customer sites, to work together on a common project. Similarly, SFR has developed a new collaborative platform for its employees, My SFR, that allows them to share their opinions on a range of issues, develop their internal network and to reveal new talents within the company.

In the not too distant future, exchange spaces such as this will be best orientated towards the sharing of ideas and decisions. Values with which employees really identify are more likely to emerge from within company communities than from head offices, which tend to impose global values that are detached from the everyday experience of employees. Management must be ready to share its prerogatives and rethink its authority. Bringing employees together through a network will also lead to an opening up of the company. This may challenge the traditional function-based organisation and mark the start of a new transverse communication channel. On an internet platform, marketing, R&D, customer services and even trade teams can gather more easily than in the physical world – especially if they are at distant geographical locations – and are empowered to work with each other to develop ideas, solutions, processes and relationships. Companies who dare to interconnect their employees and have them participate in the decision-making process will give them a real confidence booster which will in the end be transmitted to their customers (see Figure 25.1).

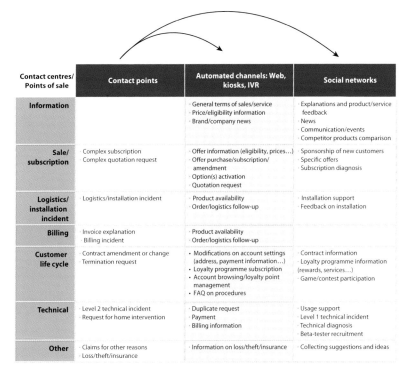

Contact centres/ Points of sale	Contact points	Automated channels: Web, kiosks, IVR	Social networks
Information		· General terms of sales/service · Price/eligibility information · Brand/company news	· Explanations and product/service feedback · News · Communication/events · Competitor products comparison
Sale/ subscription	· Complex subscription · Complex quotation request	· Offer information (eligibility, prices…) · Offer purchase/subscription/ amendment · Option(s) activation · Quotation request	· Sponsorship of new customers · Specific offers · Subscription diagnosis
Logistics/ installation incident	· Logistics/installation incident	· Product availability · Order/logistics follow-up	· Installation support · Feedback on installation
Billing	· Invoice explanation · Billing incident	· Product availability · Order/logistics follow-up	
Customer life cycle	· Contract amendment or change · Termination request	• Modifications on account settings (address, payment information…) • Loyalty programme subscription • Account browsing/loyalty point management • FAQ on procedures	· Contract information · Loyalty programme information (rewards, services…) · Game/contest participation
Technical	· Level 2 technical incident · Request for home intervention	· Duplicate request · Payment · Billing information	· Usage support · Level 1 technical incident · Technical diagnosis · Beta-tester recruitment
Other	· Claims for other reasons · Loss/theft/insurance	· Information on loss/theft/insurance	· Collecting suggestions and ideas

Figure 25.1 Customer contacts that can be automated
(source BearingPoint)

Align your employees
for maximum consistency

ORGANISATIONS THAT UNDERSTAND WHAT IT
TAKES TO DELIVER AN EXCEPTIONAL CUSTOMER
EXPERIENCE KNOW THE IMPORTANCE OF
CONSISTENCY AND HOW HARD IT IS TO ACHIEVE.

M any organisations fail when it comes to understanding their customers. They use their intuition for finding out their customers' needs and experiences, instead of analysing customer information they often have at hand. In addition, today's consumers are more sophisticated and more willing to explore alternatives to products and services that really add value, and how they are delivered. Getting closer to customers and effectively responding to their needs is a great way to boost loyalty and encourage deeper business relationships. It is also an essential part of running a organisation that wants to differentiate itself from its competitors.

Customer Experience Management (CEM) has become the new critical differentiator that organisations apply in order to create a sustainable competitive advantage. According to Hamel and Prahalad,[1] the objective is to amaze customers by anticipating and fulfilling their unarticulated needs and wants. In other words, organisations have to "wow!" their target customers; they have to exceed their expectations on critical touch points for the customer and the organisation in order to differentiate.

The next competitive battleground

With products and services becoming commoditised, creating and managing a unique customer experience is widely predicted to be the next competitive battleground. Moreover, where products and services are easily copied by competitors, delivering a customer experience that is in line with the organisation's values and brand promises is much harder. This requires organisations to differentiate by consistently exceeding the physical and emotional expectations of their customers, thereby creating a unique customer experience.

A successful organisation creates customer experiences by embedding the fundamental value proposition consistently in its offerings' every feature and on every channel. BMW, for example, clearly communicates what their customers can expect from them. A good value proposition is key because it sets the expectation and, equally important, it sets the behaviour standard of the employees of that organisation in engaging with customers.

Pike Place Fish Market in Seattle has established a reputation for having a creative environment that fosters intense employee loyalty as well as customer satisfaction. "We want to give employees and customers the best experience they've ever had" (Yokoyama).[2] Pike Place proves that an organisation comes to life when it treats its staff as peers rather than as peons. And when an organisation comes to life, the customers will follow. In differentiating by exceeding customers' expectations, the quality and scope of the service provided are important as well. For example, the tracking and shipping support FedEx provides on the internet and by phone is as important to customers as its fundamental value proposition of on-time delivery.

Consistency is key

People's expectations are partly set by their previous experiences with an organisation's offerings. Customers instinctively compare each new experience, positive or otherwise, with previous ones and make judgements accordingly. The remembrance of price, packaging, convenience and service are subject to being outmatched by the competition, but it is about the complete and consistent experience. Key here is that what persists over time – the emotional or psychological consequences of the experience, not the experience per se. Remembering a past experience produces brain activity similar to that which transpired during the actual experience. This makes it possible for organisations to help customers relive experiences.

Every time an organisation and a customer interact, the customer learns something about the organisation that will either strengthen or weaken their future relationship, and that customer's desire to return, spend more and recommend. CEM is about identifying each of these moments of truth and ensuring that the organisation, its people, products, processes and culture are aligned both strategically and tactically across all touch points to best serve the customer, based on what is most important to that customer. To put it simply, CEM is the process of strategically managing a customer's entire experience with a product or a company (Schmitt).[3]

CEM is about having a broad view of how an organisation/brand and its products and/or services can be relevant to a customer's life. It is about consistently living up to the expectations of the organisation's brand's customers. CEM also takes an integrative approach to the organisation, looking internally as well as externally. Organisations typically have an inside-out approach to serving their customers, but with CEM a switch towards an outside-in approach is crucial in understanding customer needs. In other words, CEM is about understanding customer expectations, employee experiences, the market-place landscape and operational delivery.

Branding the experience

Branding the experience involves organisations creating an experience for target customers and then branding it accordingly. Here the brand must be seen as the sum of experiences customers have across all touch points, where the crucial touch points for the brand are experience peaks and the main drivers for the customer to perceive the brand in the way the company wants it to. CEM is not effective unless it is branded. Only when you're branded can you differentiate.

To optimise the branded experience, organisations have to deliver the most unique brand values and meet or exceed the most critical needs and expectations of customers by "peak & end" experiences. Organisations can deliver a branded customer experience because they excel in two significant areas (Driggs and Piotroski):[4]

1. They rigorously include customers' voices in the process, as well as measure the delivery of the experience on an ongoing basis. This enables them to understand the key levers/touch points in the experience, what opportunities for improvement exist and what impact these changes will have on customer loyalty.
2. They operationalise these insights to ensure the customer experience is delivered consistently, across the organisation and time after time, regardless of how, or when, the customer interacts with the company.

The department store Nordstrom holds a reputation for customer service that many organisations attempt to emulate. Organisations are proud when they are compared or are called the "Nordstrom" of their industry. Nordstrom's only rule to employees is to use good judgement. Nordstrom is one of the few large organisations that truly trusts its employees to do the right thing for the customer. This creates a culture in which workers feel free to take the initiative and be creative when interacting with customers and solving problems. Nordstrom has been rated the number one in customer experience for years and is the benchmark for customer service excellence (e.g. The Nordstrom Way).

Customer experience as a competence

The power of experience-based differentiation is that it addresses the problem of retaining/increasing satisfaction and converting it into loyalty. It creates the organisation's character and uniqueness, delivering unique brand values and meeting and/or exceeding critical needs and expectations of customers at peak & end experiences. With experienced-based differentiation, organisations can improve their brand equity, their employee equity and their customer's equity. In short, obsess about customer needs not product features, and reinforce brands with every interaction through every channel, not just communications – i.e. make promises and keep/exceed promises, and treat customer experience as a competence not a function.

Organisations cannot control the entire experience, but what they can control (e.g. quality and consistency) should make quite an impression with clear implications for tracking the customer experience across each touch point and making sure that a single negative experience does not damage a hard-earned relationship. For organisations with multiple customer touch points, consistency is achieved one experience at a time. To be successful, organisations should commit to CEM. If organisations design experiences that start with customer behaviour and then infuse it with emotions and feelings, overall effectiveness will improve across all touch points. That is what differentiates good performers from average performers.

Notes

1. Hamel and Prahalad (1994).
2. Yokoyama (2000).
3. Schmitt (2003).
4. Driggs and Piotroski (2006).

RELATE
in a social
environment

Manage your e-reputation

AS A NEW SOURCE FOR ECONOMIC INTELLIGENCE
AND A MEANS OF MONITORING THE DEVELOPING
PUBLIC IMAGE OF THE BUSINESS, WEB
TRACKING HAS BECOME INDISPENSABLE.

"If you upset your customers in the real world, they are likely to tell six friends each. On the internet, your unhappy customers can tell 6,000 friends each" explains Jeff Bezos, CEO of Amazon.[1] The challenges couldn't be clearer! Just as in politics or the military, it has become essential to set up web tracking posts in businesses too.

To ensure rapid reaction, tracking is increasingly being entrusted to dedicated teams in the company. The internet's word-of-mouth effect encourages companies to be vigilant to pick up, if not control, the essence of what is being said about them. Attempts to contain surfers' opinions on monitored websites have not prevented the outbreak of "unofficial" initiatives (e.g. the "#" tag on Twitter or customer-created blogs).

However, the aim of web tracking is not only to be defensive. Businesses can exploit tracking of cybercommunities for their economic intelligence. This legal "wiretapping" is an opportunity to glean information on their markets and competitors. Brands can also use it to anticipate trends or tap into inspiration for product development, as the forums are overflowing with ideas. Finally, observing a community helps to decipher its language and then reuse it in communication.

Tracking 200 million sites is no longer enough

According to an estimate by the Netcraft research institute, in April 2010 there were 205 million sites on the web. To reduce the volume of data to be analysed, the first recommendation is to make a list of keywords to be tracked and sites to be monitored. Remember that in addition to normal sites, tracking also has to cover the comments left by 400 million Facebook users and 10 billion "tweets". How can we ignore the social networks when Facebook's launch of Open Graph is liable to plant millions of "Like" buttons all over the web, identifying brands recommended by surfers? Finally, monitoring must be kept in proportion to the legitimacy of the author of the comment. Three sources of information can be identified on the web: opinion leaders (press sites, institutional sites in your sector), upcoming intermediaries (highly ranked personal blogs) and waning or silent intermediaries (blogs read only by their authors).

Fortunately there are tools, even if they aren't perfect, for web tracking. For example, Google Alert offers free tracking based on keywords; Omniture and Digimind can be used to analyse surfers' opinions and feelings about a brand or product; Augure offers tools to analyse the impact of communication campaigns on the business's reputation. Personalised search engines such as Google Personal Search and Microsoft FAST, once set up, pick out the background trends and weak signals from the flood of contributions. There are also tracking professionals (specialist service providers, site moderators, audience analysts and community facilitators).

Tracking is good, but reacting is better

To exploit the wealth of material collected from the internet, a business needs to create bridges between its monitoring unit and its operational departments. Knowing what's being said about you on the web is of little use if it doesn't trigger any reaction. Bridges need to be short to allow you to react quickly and, for example, to defuse a conflict situation and prevent it from spiralling into damaging press.

One example is Eurostar, which, following the train breakdowns that occurred between 18 and 21 December 2009, suffered the wrath of internet users. From 18 December thousands of messages of complaint appeared on blogs and social networks. Eurostar made an emergency call to a communications agency to deal with this and to help them to respond to all of its customers. Crises can also arise out of class actions, such as those initiated by Greenpeace against Nestlé in March 2010. At that time, the role of the "community manager" was discussed at length as one element of a strategy to adapt organisational structure to effectively manage the relationship with communities.

Your employees can be your best champions

However large it may be, a tracking unit will never be able to see everything and answer the thousands of comments posted every day by surfers. Businesses therefore need more online champions, and employees can do this. Their enrolment into the tracking unit requires a number of organisational measures. First, marketing need to define the strategy and the level of intervention on social networks; secondly human resources need to determine a reward structure for employees who get involved; and finally IT need to authorise access to social networks and incorporate new tools in the workstations.

Become an influential player on the web

The best way of all to control your reputation is to build it yourself! This is possible, provided you know where and when to do it. Information generally moves around the web passing through three areas: releases (blogs, newspapers, press agencies, etc.); media coverage (aggregators, online information sites); and mobilisation (social networks, forums, etc.). It generally lands in the "grass roots" impact area (Wikipedia and search engines). This is where the discussions about businesses make their mark. A brand has to cover all these areas to be influential on the web.

A good example is the promotion by a pharmaceuticals laboratory of a slimming pill in 2009. It circulated a study on obesity to specialist journalists (release area); who then started a debate on the subject (media coverage area); and the laboratory then tracked the forums that dealt with the topic to collect the Facebook profiles of the surfers supporting its operation (mobilisation area). The operation concluded with the launch of a communications campaign about the product. This strategy enabled the offering to be launched directly to interested consumers, following a debate initiated and monitored by the laboratory. This kind of strategy, which targets all the areas (on and even off the web), is known as "control of the hub". Today it extends beyond the scope of business, with communications advisers to country leaders keen on it too.

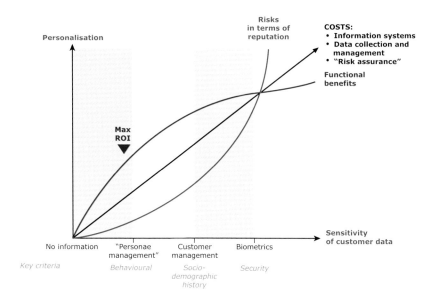

Figure 27.1 Maximise ROI in your information management
(source BearingPoint)

Note

1. Source: article on "Online Reputation" (www.digimind.com).

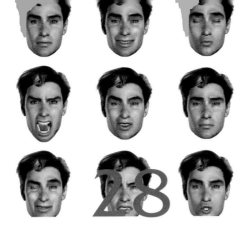

Get ready to talk with avatars

PSEUDONYMS, AVATARS, MULTIPLE EMAIL ADDRESSES … TRYING TO IDENTIFY A CUSTOMER ON THE INTERNET IS BECOMING HAZARDOUS. RATHER THAN FORCING INDIVIDUALS TO IDENTIFY THEMSELVES, SOME COMPANIES HAVE CHOSEN TO JOIN IN THE GAME AND HAVE INTRODUCED AVATARS TO TALK WITH CUSTOMERS ON AN EQUAL FOOTING.

B y 2011, it is forecast that 80% of web users will have at least one avatar at their disposal on the web. If this proves true, it introduces an additional headache for the customer relationship manager. It was already difficult enough to identify an individual hidden behind an IP address (especially when all family members are using the computer in turn), so imagine the number of people that can hide behind the same virtual identity on the internet! Especially as this identity can take several forms: from the ordinary pseudonym to the avatar made of 3D pixels!

The web world is far more transitory and less peaceful than the real world, where everyone's identity is theoretically unique and certified by official documents. Authenticating web users is a real challenge. Brands must now manage a hybrid customer relationship, between virtual worlds and reality, with all the continuity and transparency problems that entails. Because of legitimacy and cost issues, they must face up to the fact that they will never be able to know everything about their "real" customer – household structure, usages, behaviours, preferences, etc. – and now the emergence of these transitional identities deepens the complexity.

"Customer identity masked by an avatar"

To make marketers' tasks even more difficult, the consumer's role online changes according to how they are using the web. People go on line for both personal and professional reasons, and can therefore be accessing either public or secure data. Each person can therefore assume multiple identities online, and in turn can be a customer, employee, group member or subject matter expert. This realm is similar to a modern version of the classic sentence *Je est un autre* ("I is someone else") by Arthur Rimbaud.

A customer?
Employee?
Subject
matter expert?
Member?
The web
user's identity
is disguised

Fortunately, technology can sometimes come to a company's aid, and many specialist firms have emerged to help companies reveal this multiplicity of digital identities. The OpenID project aims to specify a standard to decentralise identification. It enables a user to authenticate their identity once and this enables them to gain access to several services. However, this kind of system requires the approval of web users, who may see it as an attempt to restrict their freedom of movement. Another even more radical solution is to resort to biometrics. As an example, imagine tiny video recorders mounted into computers and recording the eye's iris in order to authenticate the user. Or perhaps some small gadgets (which already exist) that identify an individual through his or her fingerprints? None of these ideas can be put into practice, however, without the cooperation of the web user.

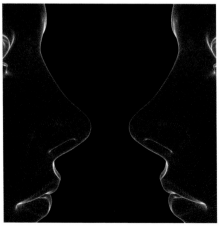

From B2C to A2A

Companies can also choose to bypass these virtual identities, or more precisely to turn them to their own advantage, by entering into the game themselves. Companies could choose to create their own avatars to communicate with web users on a level playing field. As a result we leave the B2C environment to enter the A2A, "Avatar to Avatar", environment. This concept has inspired the automotive manufacturer, Jeep, to create a character on its Facebook group page encouraging users to get in touch with the firm in an original way.

Other brands have taken this concept even further, and have begun to appear in the virtual reality world of Second Life. Second Life is actively used by 15 million people throughout the world, and does exactly what it says on the box – it gives people an opportunity to live a second life. This world allows companies to express themselves in very inventive ways. Peugeot has presented one of its "concept cars" in Second Life, while its competitor, Toyota, has gone even further by testing its *Scion xB* using the site. Some companies, such as L'Oréal, have also used Second Life for real-world recruiting purposes, while the Hollywood major, Fox, broadcast its film *XMen 3* as a preview through this medium. This parallel world is an opportunity for customer relationship management, but its commercial future is still to be proven, although the opportunity exists for brands to user-test new products and concepts for a modest sum. Companies can find a sample of customers – admittedly not always representative – on which they can conduct complete marketing studies with qualitative interviews and surveys.

Second Life no longer holds the monopoly on virtual reality as avatars have escaped to "live" on companies' institutional and trade websites too. Nowadays there are countless examples of these animated characters who "humanise" the relationship by welcoming customers and answering their questions. The hostess of BT.com is called Emma, the SNCF equivalent introduces herself as Léa, while Castorama gives life to a whole group of friends: Béa manages the decoration

section, Leïla the DIY, Jeanne the building materials and Florence the gardening. Women, in each case. Avatars are also being used in more traditional channels such as in stores. Tessa (the TExt and Sign Support Assistant), has been developed in collaboration with the UK Post Office to translate the post office clerks' verbal communication into sign language to meet the needs of people who are deaf or hard of hearing.

There are also some examples of customers and brands interacting through avatars as the intermediary, and this is likely to become commonplace in the future. Companies will be tempted to find out who hides behind the mask: a customer, a prospect, an expert, a competitor? Without specific insights, companies must always ensure they treat this avatar "customer" well to ensure it becomes a promoter rather than a detractor. Customer relationship management in virtual worlds also has its rules.

Leverage your social networks

WHILE IT IS IMPERATIVE THAT ALL ORGANISATIONS SHOULD
BE CONSIDERING HOW TO INCORPORATE SOCIAL MEDIA IN
THEIR COMMUNICATIONS AND MARKETING STRATEGIES, IT IS
ALSO VITAL THAT ANY OUTCOME IS THE RESULT OF ALIGNING
CUSTOMER STRATEGY WITH CUSTOMER BEHAVIOUR.

A successful social media strategy should be global to enhance overall brand strategy to gauge and react to how your network is talking to you, about you and what your network wants from you. Get this right and social media moves from a marketing channel to a potential sales channel, and it becomes relevant across the entire purchasing life cycle.

The use of social media in the context of co-creation, social marketing and even for driving consumer reviews is well established, and the emergence of social media as a distinct sales and service channel completes the picture. Known as f-commerce, examples are already emerging of effective use of social media channels. For example, Procter & Gamble sold 1,000 diapers within the first hour of its "f-store" opening on Facebook.

Social networks, whether online or off, are one of the most powerful ways of driving advocacy, often perceived directly impacting positive and negative experiences than interacting directly with the brand. The beauty of online social networks is the greater ability for companies to listen to the chatter and then influence the debate – and of course to inspire or instigate the discussion in the first place. Once organisations are confident that they have the ability to analyse their context-relevant social media chatter, the opportunity arises to open up the channel to direct sales using very targeted product offers. By their very nature, social media brand advocates are raising their hand as potential consumers.

Let your network speak

The ability to influence any given social network, and also to be able to target the right message across the purchase life cycle, is enabled through the ability to listen to and analyse what the network is saying.

Of course, sometimes listening doesn't take too much specialist skill, as United Airlines have discovered through the 10 million hits that the "United Breaks Guitars" video has attracted on YouTube. Domino's and Amazon have also been subjected to negative messages via social media, Amazon being deemed unresponsive for not communicating on an issue raised via Twitter within a day.

The results of listening to and analysing an individual's digital footprint across all social media can be used to drive targeted interaction, marketing messages, sales and customer account servicing right across the purchase life cycle (see Figure 29.1). Using social media as a channel into mobile and fixed internet is a key strategy to gain access to the connected community and to drive advocacy, as well as providing a way to measure customer satisfaction while distributing offers and marketing messages. A clear example of the perceived value of this comes from the $650 million drop in Netflix share value when Warner opened up a Facebook movie rental (streaming) service in 2011.

There are growing examples of social media applications being used as a "direct to" consumer sales channel. For example, Wow Bao, a Chicago-based Lettuce Entertain You Enterprise, Inc. restaurant has an "Online Ordering" tab on its Facebook page that allows "fans" to order their takeout or delivery meal right from the social media site. In another example, Sainsbury's recipe sharing becomes a direct sales channel. For example, a customer can click "I want to make this" and they automatically have all ingredients in their basket on the website, or they can get a pre-printed/texted shopping list with a marketing promotion/coupon printed on it to use at a Sainsbury's supermarket.

In Nordstrom shops, sales representatives are encouraged to use Twitter to develop loyalty and keep the after-sales link with customers. It is a way to give advices, share news, interesting website links (e.g. How to Wear a Plaid Suit)... and also to send a personal invitation to customers (http://twitter.com/nordstromdave#). Sumeet Jain of CMEA Capital predicts that "It's a matter of time – within the next five or so years – before more business will be done on Facebook than Amazon". Whether Facebook retains its current position as social network of

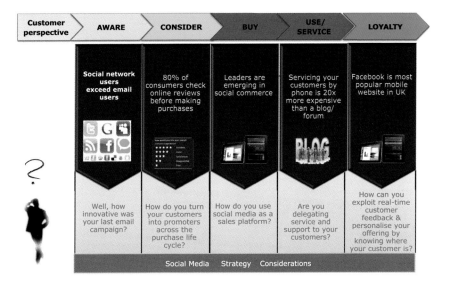

Customer perspective	AWARE	CONSIDER	BUY	USE/SERVICE	LOYALTY
	Social network users exceed email users	80% of consumers check online reviews before making purchases	Leaders are emerging in social commerce	Servicing your customers by phone is 20x more expensive than a blog/forum	Facebook is most popular mobile website in UK
	Well, how innovative was your last email campaign?	How do you turn your customers into promoters across the purchase life cycle?	How do you use social media as a sales platform?	Are you delegating service and support to your customers?	How can you exploit real-time customer feedback & personalise your offering by knowing where your customer is?

Social Media   Strategy   Considerations

Figure 29.1 Should you continue to launch email campaigns?
(source BearingPoint)

choice remains to be seen (Friends Reunited anybody? MySpace?) but Facebook's evolution from teenage chatroom to communications portal, news aggregator and now B2C commerce engine has been rapid indeed. The power of advocacy from friends and family cannot be overlooked, which, along with the ability to build a more complete picture of one's customers likes and dislikes, makes tapping into social media as a significant and focused B2C channel compelling.

Location, location, location

Taking this a stage further, knowing your customer's or prospect's location lets you complete a profile, allowing you to use virtual connections to provide real-life connections.

According to Gartner, smartphone sales are increasing at a rate of 100% per year – even in the depths of the recession. Going hand-in-hand with the explosion in smartphone usage is an increase in connectivity via mobile broadband. Better and faster networks are being developed and rolled out, for example Long-Term Evolution (LTE), LTE Advanced and 4G, meaning that the stage is set for global broadband access to become a reality. Morgan Stanley predict that by 2015 more people will connect to the internet via smartphones than via a PC. Always connected, always available, the consumer of tomorrow will expect location-based and social network relevant messages.

As an example, Facebook is the most popular mobile website in the UK, with Foursquare, the location-based social network, already integrated. Vouchercloud provides location-based offers, but these are not made with any reference to the recipient's preferences. Combining knowledge of the consumer's social network with knowledge of their location opens up a world of opportunities. At the same time, these opportunities also attract a host of new privacy risks and concerns from not only clients, but also from employees and government regulators. Social media strategies need to take these elements into consideration – listen, but listen carefully and appropriately.

As organisations develop and evolve their social media strategies, they need to be conscious of both the opportunities that the new technologies provide, as well as managing the risks and pitfalls that also present themselves. What organisations can't afford to do, however, is to drop the idea of having a social media strategy or to limit it to the established end of the purchase life cycle and to believe that consumers do not want to make purchases or request service through their social networks. They are already doing it.

What will be the next steps for companies in social media?

The question for companies is no longer whether or not to have a social media strategy but rather to define what they should do and how fast.

As a matter of fact, social media are said to be the next "phone" (immediate interaction) and will soon be the main inbox (cornerstone of all incoming informations – see Google Buzz). Beyond the facts, customers are already on social media, it is a nonsense for a company to try to escape from social media when that same company equips its employees with smartphones, emails and phones…

No emergency exists

Between one-fifth and one-quarter of all web content is behind the walls of social media platforms and remains almost invisible to traditional search engines. Moreover, no standard platform currently exists, and, for example, a Nokia and an iPhone user cannot be connected. There is therefore a key challenge for companies to manage their presence within social media walls. Louis Vuitton or GM manage for example to deliver added value to customers. As a result, they concentrate customer comments on their walls rather than on unknown and invisible ones.

In term of technical trends, search engine are expected to improve their capacities and social media aggregation tools will become more and more mature to overcome technical platform differences. The deployment of platforms like "Chatter" from Salesforce.com will help to reinforce real-time collaboration inside and outside the company. Companies will enter a new age – a B2B2C (Business to Business to Customer) social media.

Leverage real-time opportunities

The question will then become how to leverage the impacts of real-time social media. By monitoring social media streams, companies will be able to go beyond usual segmentation and to determine purchase intention – in real time. Solutions (e.g. www.compasslabs.com) will become more and more sophisticated as far as real-time segmentations on social media are concerned. For example, companies will be able to manage real-time segmentations that will impact the purchase life cycle.

For instance, companies have the opportunity to search social media and find which customers are looking for a car, already own a compact and have recently tweet on environmental issues. Another example given by Compasslabs is the opportunity to identify families fan of water sports and posting questions on vacation or even owners of smartphones and tablets, interested in sports and that have downloaded at least two applications.

Real time implies instant reaction and therefore reduces the time for testing solutions, services and approaches. Chief Marketing Officers (CMOs) will have to accept errors and misunderstandings. As far as transparency and open discussions structured the relationship with customers the impacts should remain be low. Moreover, successful management of dissatisfied customers provides a great opportunity to reinforce the relationship.

Be sure to be at the right side of the wall and establish a win-win relationship with customers

Innovate in the relationship through social media

In April 2011 the first Facebook movie – *Him, Her, Them* – was launched. Having used social media to finance a movie project, or publicise it, we are now in an era where Facebook becomes a distribution channel and a storytelling device, mixing up video, all-ready written story and add-ons directly from fans. "It aims to add a social layer to the experience of watching a movie, similar to what Zing has done with gaming" said a movie representative. It will be interesting to see how CMO might re-use this idea. Companies could present a purchase life cycle video and ask brand fans to add new interactions, services and experience at each step of a customer journey. It is another way to involve customers and enrich brand/customer experience.

Beyond all these examples, the ability to know where, when and how deep the usage of social media should be in the customer journey will be a key differentiator. For instance, using social media as a help-desk service is getting more and more mature. But it does not mean that every social media initiative offers a return on investment. Companies should measure carefully the expected impacts to guarantee a "happy end" for their social media investments.

Liven up your fan club

EVERY BRAND HAS FAITHFUL CUSTOMERS, READY TO STAND
UP FOR THE BRAND, TO PROMOTE IT TO OTHER CONSUMERS
OR EVEN TO GET INVOLVED IN ITS EVOLUTION. SOME FIRMS
CHOOSE TO GIVE THIS AUTHORITY AND RESPONSIBILITY
TO THEIR CUSTOMERS WITHIN THE CONTEXT OF
COMMUNITIES, EVEN IF THAT MEANS TAKING SOME RISKS.

Two million people contributed to a Danette (part of Danone Group) initiative to elect a new flavour for their cream desserts in France. This level of participation is more akin to expectations for a rock star's fan club than a site for yoghurt consumers! As a point of interest, it was the "Brownie" flavour that won and is now sold in supermarkets. In the UK, Walker's Crisps launched the "Do Yourself a Flavour" campaign where the creator of the winning flavour won £50,000 as well as 1% of future sales of that flavour.

Marketers from Danone and Walker's, like many others, have understood the interest of this internet buzz at a time when securing the loyalty of customers has become difficult in the face of aggressive competition and the ease with which customers can chose to switch suppliers. There is a new dimension now to gaining customer loyalty. Firms no longer seek to gain loyalty by a "push" method alone. Instead they seek to identify those people who appreciate their products and services and then convert them into ambassadors for the brand.

These ambassadors are especially valuable to a company in today's digital age, as consumers seem to place more trust in the voice of a fellow consumer than in that of the media or promotional advertising, even though that consumer is anonymous. This is illustrated by a European study conducted by Médiamétrie in December 2010, which shows that 54% of customers admit to reading evaluations expressed by other customers before they buy, and that 37.5% of those abandon the idea of buying the product because of negative evaluations.[1]

Branded or non-branded communities?

So what is the best strategy for interacting with these communities? On the one hand, communities can be created from scratch by the brands themselves (as in the case of Danette and Walker's). The advantage of this approach is it makes it easy to identify opinion makers, as they give information along with their profile. Another option is to map onto an existing blog or forum in which the brand name is mentioned. The main challenge is to identify which communities are actively discussing your brand on the internet. Software exists to scan the web and watch what is being said about your brand. There is no way of quantifying the buzz (how many key-words used, frequency of quotes, etc.), but it is possible to obtain a qualitative analysis of customer experience.

The next step is to identify opinion leaders in these communities. Not all contributors to the community will have the same level of influence. It won't necessarily be the customers who post the highest volume of content or even the most frequent site visitors. Something all opinion makers have in common, however, is their ability to attract customers by sharing their positive experiences and reassuring others who hesitate to do so. The internet service provider Free has grouped all of its opinion makers into a community that speaks highly of its service in order to concentrate positive comment.

Market research firm Forrester has listed five attitudes that companies can take towards relating with communities that discuss their brand. The scale is based on the level of intervention taken by the brand. These attitudes are: listening (customer feedback); discussion (brand communication); stimulation (generating recommendations); encouragement (promoting in a way that mutually aids brand and customer); and rallying (involving customers in a co-creation process). The UK government, for example, has played the "stimulation" card by enabling citizens to post their opinions on upcoming legislation, and local government bodies have a site system called "Have Your Say". An example of the "encouragement" intervention, where there is mutual aid for the brand and customer, is Amazon Vine, developed by Amazon.co.uk. Through this programme a select group of Amazon customers are able to post opinions about new and pre-release items to help fellow customers make educated purchase decisions. In exchange, Vine members are provided with free copies of products that have been submitted to the programme by publishers or manufacturers.

Treat ambassadors like VIPs

Whatever way these firms identify and communicate with these active consumers, compensation must be taken into account. The people who actively contribute to blogs and forums appreciate being listened to, and enjoy the attention that comes with recognition. It is vital therefore for the brand to further engage these people, and invite them to make recommendations to other community members via commentary, or even by directly answering questions. In effect, this is making these individuals spokespersons for the brand. Brands could take this even further and use these customers to test future products and find out their opinion on what works. Finally, brands can even consider compensating these contributors in cash, as in the Walker's case mentioned earlier.

Organising a community is no small feat. It requires both internet technical savvy and round-the-clock dedicated resource as posts cannot be left for long without a response. The brand has to demonstrate that it is actively involved with the community by listening and responding to comments. However, the poor perception created by slow responses to blogs is not the worst consequence a company may face. The risk of seeing the firm's brand value drop and financial performance suffer as a result of a bad comment is far more serious. One negative review can undo all of the benefits accumulated from a series of positive reviews. Furthermore, negative opinions are often better classified on search engines, where they can remain visible for months. Therefore, companies who do open themselves up to comment on the internet and give consumers a voice on their websites can open themselves up to risk. There is also a risk of sabotage; competitors or malicious individuals may well post information. It will always be difficult to protect oneself against this type of behaviour (see Figure 30.1).

In a context where everything can be said and read, the only steadfast rule is *transparency towards consumers* – especially opinion leaders, who could become detractors if they felt they had been betrayed by the brand. An important European

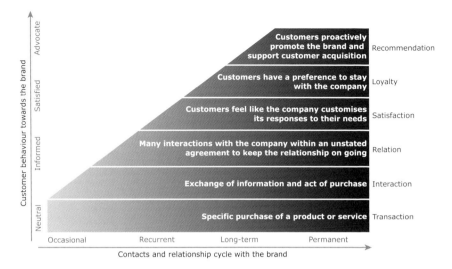

Figure 30.1 Communities make customer promoters stronger and more valuable (source BearingPoint)

bank has borne the brunt of this, when it was attacked by students on Facebook in protest at its decision to remove interest-free credit post-graduation from university. The smear campaign was so successful that the bank reversed its policy decision. The lesson this bank learned is that a fan club has to be deserved.

Note

1.   Médiamétrie (2010). *The Observatory of Internet Usage.*

31

Work out what drives your customers to become promoters or detractors

HAVING A GOOD EXPERIENCE WITH A BRAND IS NOT ALWAYS
ENOUGH TO MAKE A CUSTOMER LOYAL TO THAT BRAND.
USUALLY A CHAIN OF POSITIVE EVENTS NEEDS TO OCCUR.

"Would you recommend our product or service to a friend?" If you have ever answered this question in a satisfaction survey it means that, without knowing it, you probably gave information intended to gauge a "recommendation score". Companies – aware of the advantage of a customer relationship driven by recommendation – are including this question in their satisfaction surveys. These scores aim to assess consumer attachment to the brand and their potential capacity to promote it. It is a great tool, and companies using it are even able to aggregate the scores in order to calculate the value of the customer portfolio.

A company can gain a more efficient score if it asks this question at several stages in the customer life cycle. The quality of such a measurement will also depend on its capacity to take loyal customers' recommendations into consideration.

This type of recommendation or promotion score is complimentary to the common customer satisfaction surveys distributed by companies, and results in a wiser multi-channel vision. The recommendation score is a useful tool for measuring the way a customer is feeling at different stages of the relationship with the

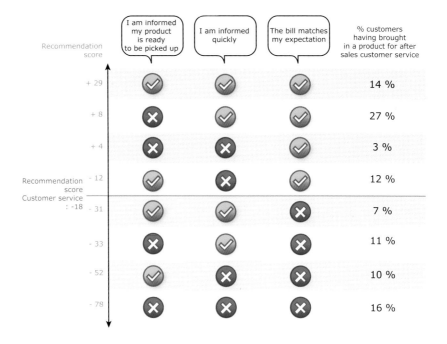

Figure 31.1 Impact of a positive or negative sequence on the recommendation score (source BearingPoint)

company, and also delivers more operational measures, which can be directly linked with the professional and financial goals of the company (see Figure 31.1).

Locate the "moment of truth"

Once implemented, this type of scoring can help companies identify the reasons behind customers becoming detractors or advocates of a brand. This can be achieved through statistical analysis of the words used by customers in their responses. Motives remain varied, from the capacity of a company to listen to its customers, to delivery times, waiting times, value for money and so on. The reasons can also differ from one channel to another (such as web or telephone). Understanding these reasons can, among other things, help companies to recognise which mechanisms they can employ to convert a customer into an advocate. Companies will benefit

Uncover the keys that turn a consumer into a promoter

from identifying the "moments of truth" in the customers' experience, when individuals are made into proponents or detractors of the brand.

Identifying the broad reason for customer dissatisfaction is often not enough, and companies need to conduct deeper analysis of the issue. One service company was aware that invoicing was an issue for customers, so it undertook steps to ensure the payment process was clear, concise, accurate and accessible. It even tried to attract environmentalists by printing invoices.

Control the chain reaction

Understanding the value of a succession of positive customer experiences is key as this can turn customers into brand promoters. Even a customer who contacts a call centre to complain can become a brand promoter if the issue is resolved in a timely and friendly manner. By contrast, a succession of poor customer experiences will fuel creation of brand detractors. For example, if prospective buyers calling to gather more information on a product are made to wait 15 minutes for unsatisfactory answers to their questions they are likely to become brand detractors.

It is critical for companies to recognise and understand the thresholds and saturation points that affect a customer's potential to promote or criticise their brand. Equipped with this knowledge, a company can work on appropriate strategies to improve its service levels. One telecommunications operator decided to ensure retention strategies were employed whenever a customer called to report a complaint. This type of analysis also aids companies in the design of their loyalty programmes, as they can begin to ask questions about whether it makes sense to concentrate rewards only on those customers who are most profitable. The recommendation is to keep analysing and investigating different options.

Digitise your loyalty programme

POINTS SCHEMES, DISCOUNT VOUCHERS AND COMPETITIONS HAVE REVEALED THEIR LIMITATIONS. NOW THAT THESE ARE FALLING OUT OF FAVOUR, "NEW GENERATION" LOYALTY STRATEGIES ARE BEING DEVISED… INCLUDING DIGITAL!

Increase the frequency of purchases and average spend by advocating service and in more unexpected ways fulfilling the individual and social conscience: Maslow is turned upside-down… More than 10 loyalty cards: that's what you find in the average consumer's wallet. We're nearly overdosing on them! And to make matters worse, most of these cards rely on a single mechanism – point reward schemes.

This concept has reached its peak over the past decade. According to a study, more than 40% of top companies now operate a loyalty scheme in the UK. There is a risk of saturation not only in the point schemes: other types of customer benefits (discounts, loyalty vouchers and competitions) have also got out of hand. Victims of their own success, they are all suffering the "spam" effect: customers are tiring of them, even complaining of being bombarded. Worse still, only 25% feel that the benefits offered are worth the bother! At the other end of the scale, businesses wonder about the efficiency of these schemes and the adverse effects of too many special offers and discounts on the value and image of their brand in the minds of customers. Harsh economic reality has even prompted some airlines to reduce the level of benefits of their reward schemes.

More service and fewer monetary benefits

To escape from this impasse, marketing managers are trying to reinvent loyalty. The challenge is to innovate through habit and the service associated with the loyalty scheme, rather than to keep offering monetary benefits. In France, Darty is the longest-standing member of the family of service-based schemes. Its customer card gives access to the electronic guarantee records of the products bought in its shops. It also allows customers to monitor orders on line and entitles them to telephone assistance and downloads of instruction manuals. Finally, by simply scanning their card in the shop, customers can for instance quickly find the right bags for their vacuum cleaner, as the card stores all their product information.

In the same spirit, Air France is carrying out research to improve customer loyalty that goes beyond ticket purchases or presence in the airport. The airline wants to know what means of transport its passengers use to get to the airport, what music they listen to on the way, or how their destination influences their state of mind and buying decisions. The answers to these questions will certainly enable them to devise new loyalty-enhancing services including advice, virtual payment, finance facilities, free delivery in retail and after-sales service – i.e. spanning the whole customer value chain. The aim is to be there every minute of the day for its customers and to simplify their lives. Nespresso has got the idea. Club Nespresso members can obtain advice from coffee specialists and can even, in an almost oracle-like operation, be notified by mail when their stocks of capsules are likely to run out!

Gaining loyalty through Twitter

But the development of services is fortunately not the only way of saving loyalty schemes. The outbreak of consumer communities, or rather interest groups, is another possibility. And of course the internet is involved.

The arrival of online consumers, blogs and forums is symptomatic of a new style of relationship between consumers, known as C2C. Social networks such as MySpace, Facebook and LinkedIn are creating an open and participative world. The recommendations and information exchanged in these groups on the use and perception of products influence members' buying behaviours and their attachment to a product or brand, almost like among family members. So-called "next generation" loyalty programmes must take account of this. Businesses are already hiring psychologists and anthropologists onto their marketing teams, and universities are supporting this trend by offering courses specialising in "consumer psychology".

Several big names in retail have gone a step further. They have built the social networks into their marketing. For instance, Starbucks, Whole Foods and Dell have decided to exploit Twitter. Every month, more than two million "statuses", snippets of life posted on the site by consumers, are filtered, studied and used to win and retain new customers. Some companies go even further. One of Europe's biggest telecommunications companies and the French postal services also opted for answering questions and comments from their users on Twitter. Maslow's hierarchy of needs that has long inspired marketing strategies has been turned upside-down! The need for recognition, friendship, to be part of a community and the need for personal achievement are coming to the fore.

This new aspiration can be exploited in many ways. The first one is to foster relationships between customers. IKEA has recently been offering a car-pooling service. Drivers use the symbol "Blah blah" in their profile to indicate that they are "happy to chat in the car". So now everyone knows that the best way to go to IKEA is to share a car! Another possibility for business: act as a "trusted third party" for the community. A player in large-scale retail might launch a platform enabling its customers to rent property to one another. The brand, the trusted third party, takes on the role of guarantor, thereby eliminating the need for tenants to pay a deposit.

The "welcome back" money-spinner

Most businesses endeavour to win new customers but neglect to win back those they have lost, on the assumption that a lost customer is gone forever! This is highly questionable. Many customers terminate a contract because they have no other choice. For example, a life-changing event or incident such as a divorce can prompt a customer to terminate an internet or telephone subscription. Telephone and energy players have launched "welcome back" operations, capitalising on a precise knowledge of their former customers to win them back. This practice, costing five to ten times less than recruiting new customers, can bring in three to four times as many new customers. Another advantage is that a returning customer will be less likely to leave again.

The digital loyalty card

There is one last way of giving new momentum to loyalty schemes. Some retailers aim to avoid the "11th loyalty card" effect by using the client's phone as the log-in app when they enter the store or pay for goods. The client who accepts the log-in at the entrance sees the promotions running; the same client can use their phone to increment their loyalty bonus. This allows personalised and real-time marketing and simplifies the customer journey – two major issues in loyalty today. It's another example of how loyalty schemes can be rejuvenated (see Figure 32.1).

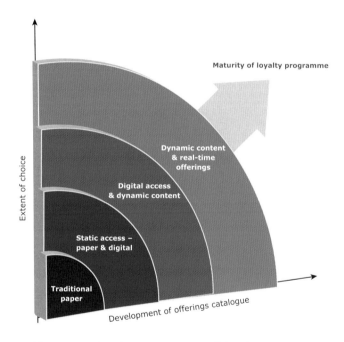

Figure 32.1 Loyalty programme model at the digital age
(source BearingPoint)

33

(Re)-win customer trust

ON THE INTERNET, AS WELL AS THROUGH OTHER
MEDIA, CUSTOMERS OPENLY CONTEST BRAND CLAIMS
IN WHICH THEY NO LONGER BELIEVE.

Companies can regain the trust of consumers through their honesty. Tactics include: stating their identity when they express themselves online; offering a mediation service; or even taking on the role of a trustworthy third party. Examples are discussed in this chapter.

The trading site eBay has built a part of its trust rating thanks to PayPal. The company, which has set the standard for the sale of goods between individuals, had the foresight to develop its own security system for online payments. Importantly, this reassured web-users at a time when security concerns were curbing people's desire to buy online. Today eBay is the global leader for sales between individuals with more than $100 billion of transactions in 2010. PayPal has even become a quality guarantee in its own right, with many trade websites relying on PayPal to run their payments and proudly displaying the PayPal logo on their front page.

In the knowledge field, the founders of Wikipedia have proved that it is possible to establish the biggest universal encyclopaedia (by volume and number of languages) with reliable information, auto checked and continuously updated, with content generated by readers themselves.

Engage with openness and honesty

These two examples prove that customer and partner trust can be won even on the internet. The days when all information sourced from the web was inevitably accompanied by suspicion are thankfully over.

Businesses operating in the physical world can also benefit from this trust rating that the internet has been able to create, although it is a recent development and still fragile. Companies like the French firm Darty, and its famous "trust contract" (*contrat de confiance*), did not wait for the emergence of Web 2.0 to differentiate its customer relationships through trust.

On the web, the first steps into 2.0 in the customer relationship management (CRM) realm were punctuated by a few blunders. Some of these unsophisticated attempts included "infiltrating" exchange websites to try to control the information, or even to use it as a commercial platform – and they all failed. One famous brand recently had to explain itself to the press regarding the content of a blog, which was claimed to be independent, but the content of which was in fact controlled by the brand itself. The brand suffered a lengthy period of criticism as a result and its brand reputation suffered. The lesson here is that, in any attempt to influence public opinion, it is better to do so openly. In the end, any efforts on behalf of brands to control everything are illusory.

Another strategy that companies can adopt is to position themselves as a trustworthy third party (see Figure 33.1). Some invite their customers to co-build their products in order to strengthen "client intimacy". For example, the French government has set up the ensemble-simplifions.fr website to collect proposals from citizens on ways to simplify administrative procedure. More than a third of the proposals were implemented in 2010! In another field Danone, via its *"Danette des régions"*, enables consumers to choose their favourite flavours through a dedicated website. A few weeks later, chosen products are produced and sold. Other businesses facilitate connections between clients. For instance, Air France launched the community "Bluenity" to link travellers present at the same time on the same itinerary.

Web opinion is more credible than corporate communications

Playing the part of the trustworthy third party can also lead more easily to favourable customer experience. Third-party websites such as tripadvisor.co.uk, which hosts commentary from customers – be it positive or negative – provides other visiting customers with a full suite of public opinion to guide their decision-making process. There is no need for these third-party "hosts" to make any comment on the customer reviews. After all, consumers have more faith in the word of their fellow customers than they do in any "official" review. The trust

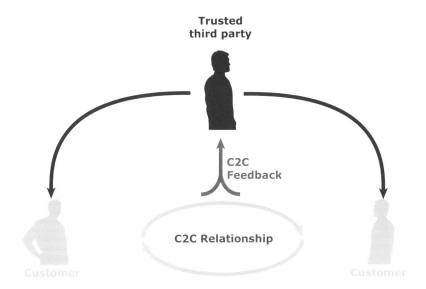

Figure 33.1 Trust is central to a customer relationship
(source BearingPoint)

rating in third-party comparison sites has increased from 20% in 2003 to 66% nowadays.[1] A large number of sites, such as Amazon.co.uk have understood this: on books they evaluate consumers' opinion on a neutral basis and release a hit-parade.

Company mediation

However, this is not to say that anonymous opinion is all-powerful. Consumer reviews will certainly help the decision-making process of someone looking to purchase a camera, for example, but practical details such as technical specifications and characteristics of the product are still very important in the final decision. Web-users' opinion just adds a human element to the decision-making process.

Furthermore, companies are not helpless in the face of virulent attacks from consumers. Some websites have begun to moderate comments about companies, and some websites are acting as mediators in the debate. Frédéric Klotz has been a pioneer of this. Since 2003, he has been known as Mr Trust in France. He runs the online trade website rueducommerce.com, and declares himself as such when

speaking on the net. He refers to himself as a "mediator/quality manager", answering customers' questions on blogs and forums which he skims every day, managing to process up to 30 opinions daily. He listens to complaints, calms the most aggressive and can even defend his employer in court in case of insoluble disputes.

Other companies have created websites where employees – whose careers are displayed on the website – commit to answer questions asked by registered web-users every day. Company channels and methods of communication are therefore moving away from pure commercial relationships and are strengthening partnership development with customers.

Finally, company strategy can be at its most efficient if its employees, first in charge of spreading the word, trust the brand they work for. It is no coincidence that companies who are successful in the web sphere (Google, Microsoft, Apple), are also in the top rankings of best places to work, reflecting their employees' trust in their company.

Note

1. Médiamétrie, *Monitoring Internet Usage & an Internet Barometer: From Fourth Trimester 2001 to Fourth Trimester 2010*.

Personalise without knowing
your customers

NOWADAYS IT IS POSSIBLE TO GET TO KNOW YOUR CUSTOMERS
WHETHER THEY LIKE IT OR NOT. THANKS TO PROGRESS WITH
ANALYSIS TECHNIQUES, BRANDS HAVE THE TOOLS TO BETTER UNRAVEL
CONSUMER BEHAVIOURS. IT'S UP TO BUSINESSES TO CAPITALISE ON
THIS TO SEND PERSONALISED OFFERS OF UNPRECEDENTED RELEVANCE.

Just imagine. You go to a website and you get a different home page from your neighbour. Sounds like science fiction? Not for much longer. Websites are working on pages that adapt automatically to the visitor. How on earth can they do that? Websites are recording (and storing) visitors' browsing data. A business has to simply correlate some statistics to deduce a web surfers' preferences from their previous visit, without having to ever know the surfer's precise identity.

Customers' actions speak louder than words

This type of deep analysis has only been possible since the arrival of the digital era. We know that the internet channel broadens the possibilities for product and service personalisation due to the detail it provides about consumers. Web tracking can be employed to gather a mine of behavioural information that can be used by businesses to build their personalisation programmes. The advantages are obvious. The source of information is no longer what customers agree to reveal of their identity and preferences (the conventional CRM approach), but what they do and how they do it, based on the concept that their actions are surely a better indicator of what they want! Previously, the only way businesses could get this close to the customer was by conducting complicated and costly qualitative analyses.

Amazon was one of the first to implement this principle, in the form of its recommendations system: "Customers who liked this item also liked...". The site cross references not only its customers' choices to suggest new products but also enriches customer journey using "clic stream" information or communities-based recommendations. And it works! Using the web tracking tool, Amazon has been able to increase sales by 25%. And again, there's no need to waste time or energy identifying or getting to know customers. Their purchases rather than their profiles speak for them (shopping cart history, wish-list analysis, recommendation history, etc.). With digital technology, the business saves years of intelligence marketing by garnering a lot of relevant information in one click.

While this principle sounds attractive, it requires two precautions and has one drawback. To start with, you have to sort through the information gathered, as web tracking generates a huge volume of data. This is a precondition for effective customer segmentation. Next, you have to be careful how you use the data to avoid any risk of the "big brother" effect, as most of this information is collected without the surfer's permission. Powerful though it may be, this personalisation model also has its limits. Because it is anonymous, it is based purely on a view of what the surfer is doing at that moment in time, and the information saved by tools – cookies – are of questionable reliability.

Digital interaction is an amazing data gathering tool and is also effective when exchanging data. Apple understood this long ago. The computer manufacturer offers customers its Genius programme to encourage them to share their digital identity with the company, from the most anodyne information such as their email address to the detailed content of their multimedia library. In doing so, Apple can take advantage of this tacit consent to make increasingly personalised offers to its customers.

Hopes for augmented reality

This is a real step forward for businesses in making more effective offers and for the consumer who receives more relevant offers, but it is not enough. Customers expect more from their relationship with the business. They want their whole experience with the brand to be personalised, beyond the product.

Nike was first to evolve in that direction. In 2009 it launched a large-scale pan-European mobile marketing campaign in which it released the Nike

PhotoID customisation service, which allowed Nike fans to submit their mobile phone-taken pictures with brilliant colours to the company. The service would then analyse and withdraw two dominant colours from the pictures, make customised trainer designs and send pictures of the designs back to the photographers, who could choose either to keep them as wallpaper or order the personalised shoes.

There are other ways of forging a closer link between consumers and the brand to encourage them to take up the product. In the tourism sector, Mtrip has decided to renew the classic (and paper) travel guide by offering their customers a real, personalised guide based on a simple selection of centre of interest and answers to a few straightforward questions. With these guides, your holiday scrapbook will be more unique. Further personalisation is achievable; a user can set what time they want alerts to arrive and what days they want to be told of problems on their route. Combining the service of both well-known brands, Nike and Mtrip, provides the user with a truly multifaceted and reliable service.

Another example is Michelin. The company has merged two of its products – the Michelin guides and Via Michelin – to offer its customers a comprehensive solution by marrying a geolocation service (personalised by nature) to its famous food reviews. With initiatives of this type, the business uses digital technology to move from the product to a more complete offering (product and service) allowing the user to read reviews of preferred restaurants in preferred locations, hence further enhancing its global reach and relationship with the user.

Very soon it will be possible to go even further thanks to "augmented reality", one of the latest manifestations of the digital revolution. Once this technology has been harnessed, it will be possible to use it to strengthen the bond between personalisation and customer experience. Using this technology, customers can personalise a product, and most of all can incorporate it into their personal environment. IKEA already allows potential customers to view how furniture would look in their homes prior to purchasing the item. The technique involves "Augmented Reality Paper", which has built-in technology to store a 3D model of the item. The shopper then places the paper on a spot where the furniture would be placed, and by viewing the paper through a camera/smartphone is able to see a 3D graphical representation of the furniture item.

When customers personalise their personalisation

The digital dimension is clearly a major lever in the development of a personalised customer relationship. This is happening in two ways: through the technologies it enables, which offer novel interaction possibilities and probably even more, and through the decisive behavioural changes that it induces in consumers. The result is that customers can choose their own personalised mode of personalisation. What are customers looking for? Personalising the products they buy, or just personalising the way they use them through additional services? Are their expectations confined to products or do they relate to the whole brand experience? Finally, do they want to identify themselves with the company or do they prefer to receive personalised offers without revealing their identity? Anything is possible, and it is up to each consumer to decide (see Figure 34.1).

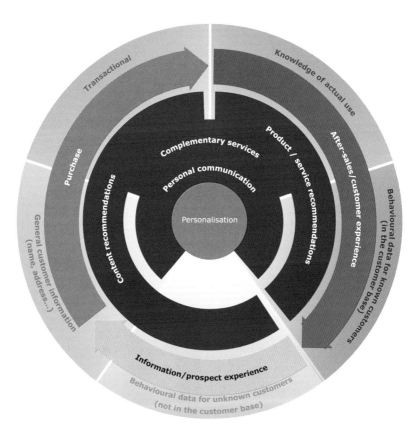

Figure 34.1 Personalisation throughout the customer life cycle (source BearingPoint)

Delegate your customer service...
to your customer

IS IT POSSIBLE TO SAVE MONEY BY DELEGATING SERVICE TO
YOUR CUSTOMERS? SOME COMPANIES HAVE MANAGED THIS
SUCCESSFULLY, AND HAVE HANDED OVER CERTAIN BASIC
CUSTOMER CARE ASPECTS TO OTHER CUSTOMERS, WHICH IS
A GOOD WAY TO RELIEVE PRESSURE ON CALL CENTRES.

Registering a customer of a company as "employee of the month" sounds rather crazy. However, in the world of participative customer relationships, this is already a topical issue. With pressure on companies to reduce their spend on their call centres, they are increasingly turning to their most engaged customers to take on some of the burden. There are three options for reducing the costs of a company service centre; companies could limit the number of special offers in order to reduce the number of incoming calls and queries; an alternative approach is to standardise some call centre operations and automate them using Interactive Voice Recognition (IVR) systems; the most original approach, however, involves calling upon user communities to deal with queries.

User communities as an alternative to call centres

Companies can take advantage of the extensive product knowledge of some of their existing customers by drawing on this knowledge to answer queries from new customers. This concept is known as "crowd-sourcing". Microsoft provides an excellent example of crowd-sourcing through its Most Valuable Professional (MVP) programme. Microsoft encourages professionals from all walks of life to share their real-world expertise voluntarily in technical communities. This helps others solve problems, discover new capabilities and get the maximum value from their technology. Contributors are awarded MVP status after a rigorous review of the quality, quantity and level of impact of the MVP nominee's contributions over the last year. In return for their efforts, MVPs are provided with access to free technical resources that enable them to further their knowledge and skills.

Benefiting from customers' expertise to support other customers

They are also given a dedicated lead contact within Microsoft whose role it is to keep the MVP up to date with special events, opportunities, seminars and news.

Microsoft has successfully developed a strategy that encourages participation, provides a forum for feedback, innovation and customer support, while at the same time providing a real incentive for the MVPs by offering them special events, training and resources. This is a dream scenario for companies for two reasons. First, as has been mentioned, customers have more faith in the word of their peers than in those of the company itself. Secondly, the sheer volume of calls for assistance cries out for this alternative method, especially as the internet is associated with being permanently accessible. It is for these reasons that this strategy is increasingly seen as a viable alternative to relying 100% on call centres.

Not all contact channels can be outsourced

There may be no technical restrictions to implementing this type of strategy, but it does require some effort. First, companies need to identify which communities will host the interaction between customers and make them more accessible. Secondly, they need to encourage influential web users and contributors to get involved in making the project a success. If the community in question forms an association naturally within a website managed by the company, it is obviously easier, because topic moderation and content exchange (and even veracity of information) will thus come under the company's control. If not, however, it is in the company's interest to join in with the forum where their product issues are being discussed.

The most effective example of this type of partnership is the internet company Free, who has taken the wise and necessary precaution of putting its customer service centre and an independent user forum in close contact. The link to this website is published on its own company website. Most interestingly, Free has managed to improve its brand reputation among the users of its web forum by establishing a close relationship with the people in charge of these websites.

Could communities be the new paradise for customer relationships? Perhaps, but it is unwise to be too rash. Some independent communities provide support while also hosting complaints and findings that can damage a company's brand reputation. Orangeproblems.co.uk is an independent website in the UK devoted to providing a community to deal with problems faced by Orange broadband users. It was born out of frustration with dealing with the company's customer service department. Although this site provides support to 11,000 users, it also shamelessly advertises that Orange was voted the worst ISP by *BBC Watchdog* in March 2007. Outsourced customer service in this case took place outside the company's control and is potentially provided at a cost. Another consideration is that customer contribution is only possible in some instances and not all support can be outsourced. It all depends on the complexity of the request being processed, on the confidential nature of the request, on the frequency of the request, and, of course, on the urgency of the request. In summary, it is frequent and basic questions whose answers do not involve a value judgement on the company that can easily be outsourced to other customers in communities. With some of the most involved web contributors, it may be possible to pass on more complex or critical requests into their hands, and indeed some companies leave it up to technophiles in their forums to trade tips on very technical issues. It can be a deliberate strategy for the company to record the answers given in the forum, and replicate them in their agent scripts at the call centre.

Refocus call centres on operations with added value

Another issue that arises is over goodwill payments. All voluntary work has its limits, and even the most motivated people could end up asking for financial compensation for the service they are effectively providing. Even so, adopting this strategy of utilising web forums is an attractive option. Companies will still experience savings as a result of reducing volumes of calls placed into their call centres. The trick is for companies to focus call centre agents on high value-added contacts (such as those driven by marketing campaigns, delay announcements, etc). The strategy is a win-win situation for companies, customers and employees alike (see Figure 35.1).

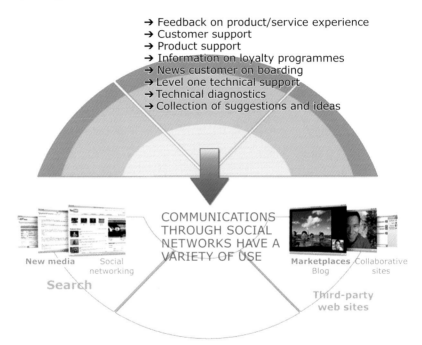

Figure 35.1 Effective use of online social networking
(source BearingPoint)

Drive your ecosystem of partners

PRODUCT AND SERVICE OFFERINGS ARE BECOMING
INCREASINGLY COMPLEX. MOST BUSINESSES USE PARTNERS TO
HANDLE THEM FROM END TO END. THE CHALLENGE HERE IS
TO BUILD A SEAMLESS RELATIONSHIP WITH YOUR PARTNERS.

Who has not felt the frustration of being sent almost like a ping-pong ball from your internet provider to your telephone operator, or even to your computer supplier, when you have a problem with your "box"? Annoyances of this kind are not confined to the phone, internet or television. These days they are found in several consumer sectors, with a growing number of businesses involved in the same product or service. For example, banks are selling mobile phone packages and online travel agencies are offering "tailor-made" holidays, including not only transport and accommodation but also activities at the resort and insurance. In order to make these offers, the banks and travel agents need to set up two-way contact with their partners.

Partnerships, the new "must have" for businesses

There is a reason for all these partnerships. Companies need them for efficiency reasons and because it is impossible to directly manage increasingly complex businesses, especially with the digital revolution. Indeed, being an actor in the digital landscape requires new skill-sets from small boutiques who often invent their job while they do it, like online buzz agencies, community website moderation agencies, e-reputation editors and so forth. These partnerships involve two or more businesses and the requester must manage a full-scale ecosystem of partners.

So far so good. The problem here is that these service providers are increasingly in contact with the final consumer at one time or another during the product's life cycle (delivery, set-up, repair, etc.), and the trouble starts when a customer complains about an incident to one of these service providers and does not get the answer they expected. Such aggrieved customers can then do serious damage to the brand (a smear campaign on the web, class action), even if the failure is the fault of one of the partners. To ward off such problems, businesses must ensure a smooth path for their customers between the different business partners.

Recommendation one: review the business's key performance indicators for its partners. Productivity and quality measurements are often written into the Service Level Agreement (SLA), but this is no longer enough. You need to consider the whole customer journey rather than simply assessing each partner individually. A poorly designed path that forces the customer to juggle with several contact points will cause a bad impression, even if each partner is faultless. The case of Superpilote.com is a good illustration of this. This site offers sports driving courses, given by a service provider, ACC. After placing an order by telephone with Superpilote, the customer receives a call from ACC asking for more information, such as the date and time of the course. As a result, the customer doesn't understand clearly who he or she is dealing with and feels that there is a lack of communication between the two partners. This can be annoying, even though both correspondents have been polite and professional. In this way the customer experience is made more complex by the involvement of the partner.

Evaluating and managing your ecosystem

Recommendation two: supplement the measurement of "quality delivered" by an indicator of "quality perceived" by the customer. Customer satisfaction is subjective and depends on individual perception of the service rather than its real value. What's more, it evolves over time. And yet it is the criterion that shapes their judgement of the brand. While "quality perceived" should not be the sole responsibility of the partners – as it is influenced by factors outside their control – measuring it nevertheless enables the business to adjust its processes throughout the whole value chain.

To clearly distinguish quality delivered from quality perceived, it is essential to introduce quality indicators. Thus the Net Promoter Score (NPS) has joined the conventional evaluation tools (mystery shoppers and recorded telephone calls). NPS is a management tool that can be used to gauge the loyalty of a firm's customer relationships. General Electric uses NPS to evaluate process excellence for its customers, and plans to use this scoring as a metric to decide the compensation of its leaders. Procter and Gamble uses NPS to measure consumer reactions to its brands and Allianz uses it to maintain what it calls "customer centricity". But looking further ahead, with the explosion of customers airing their views on the internet the "e-reputation" score must now be included in this tool.

Once the measurement tools are in place, the business has to devise an organisation that will allow it to manage its service providers in a professional way, such as setting up a dedicated department – a step several businesses have now taken. They select the partners, sign the contracts and monitor their services from end to end. These departments rely on formal evaluation processes that enable them to compare the service provided by the partners to make them more uniform. To deliver a quality customer experience, the business also has to do more than co-operate with and monitor its service providers. While the term is often bandied about, some businesses do succeed in making it meaningful again. Nowadays no one thinks of contact centre outsourcers as ordinary service providers any more. They have developed value chain skills that are complementary to those of their requesters. They even persuade their customers to get more involved in the internet, when they offer new services such as facilitating online communities. They have won their spurs as partners and are now a fully fledged part of the requester's ecosystem (see Figure 36.1).

Building a seamless customer relationship

Integrating partners and getting them to evolve in the desired direction requires some effort. You need at least to pass on your business's values and processes. This is what a specialist retail group is doing by inviting its partners to participate in "immersion" courses. This simple and inexpensive exchange offers an advantage for the future, as it helps to limit differing practices and contradictory messages to customers.

Deal with your partners' failings

After working on the basics, the communication tools need to be fine-tuned. The new dematerialised partnerships call for shared information systems. In the age of digitised exchanges and the proliferation of terminals (smartphones, interactive tables, etc.), interoperability must be guaranteed around common architecture. Thus Orange uses exchange platforms via APIs, which facilitate the transfer of customer information from one site to another. The solution is more efficient for the partners and offers a real benefit for customers who complete the transaction without having to identify themselves several times.

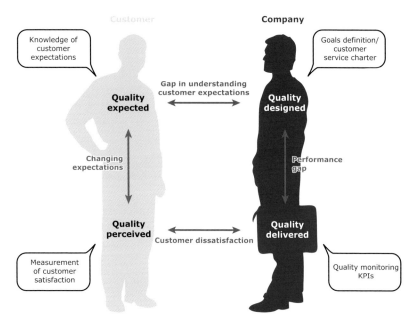

Figure 36.1 Measuring quality
(source BearingPoint)

In the digital age, customers' expectations are clear: they want a harmonised service and a clear path to follow. For businesses, the challenge is just as clear in terms of customer relations: to deliver! In other words, to take responsibility for and resolve incidents, even if they are a partner's fault. Ebay has understood this. The site has established a top-level assistance hotline for traders who sell through its shopping gallery. The benefit for customers is immediate: they can contact one single person whatever the brand concerned. This is how businesses need to operate to build a seamless customer pathway and thus a successful relationship (see Figure 36.2).

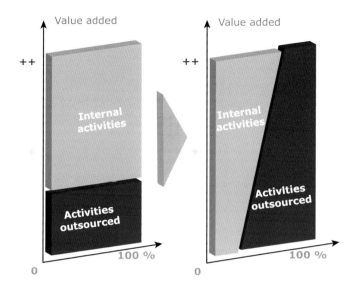

Figure 36.2 Evolution over time of activities entrusted to outsourcers (source Bearingpoint)

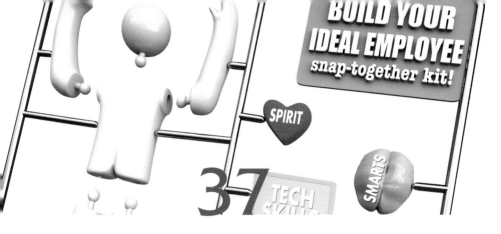

Empower your employees

"EMPLOYEE EMPOWERMENT" IS SAID TO BE THE NEW LEVER
FOR INNOVATION IN CUSTOMER MANAGEMENT, BUT WHAT
DOES IT REALLY MEAN AND DOES IT REALLY IMPART A "WOW!"
EFFECT FOR CUSTOMERS? WHAT ARE THE KEY SUCCESS
FACTORS OF AN EMPLOYEE EMPOWERMENT STRATEGY?

"Employee empowerment" encapsulates the idea of reconnecting employees and customers, and recognising the key role of employees in customer relationships. As a paradox, the more digital the world becomes, the more companies should focus on human relationships and employee initiatives to strengthen the "Wow!" effect for the customer.

The concept values the idea that employees can bring an innovative approach, and that they have the ability to directly solve problems and transform customers into ambassadors at each critical moment of the customer journey. It may sound obvious but it is not that easy, implying as a minimum:

1. Accepting a shift in the power game.
2. Understanding how to generate a "Wow!" effect through employee empowerment.
3. Reducing the "employee digital divide".
4. Imagining a new management approach benefiting from employee empowerment.

Accept a shift in the power game

Customers have never been more powerful than today. They are over-connected and over-informed "anytime, anywhere, through any device, to anybody…". Thanks to social networks, over-connected customers have the power to undermine a brand. Even government have cause for concern: social media did not cause the revolutions in Tunisia or Egypt in early 2011, but they clearly enabled citizens to have a voice and to influence events (*BBC Newsnight*, January 2011).

The self-care approach and simplicity programmes designed to reduce costs have in fact transferred complexity from employees to customers. Self-care programmes aim to place tasks usually carried out by employees into the hands of customers. For example, a digital platform can enable customers to manage their bank accounts or telco services (e.g. BforBank or Vodafone SFR). A simplicity programme will make sure the offering is easy for the customer to understand, compare, buy and use. If a company combines self-care and simplicity approaches, employees may be less equipped, less well-informed and less trained than customers. At least customers, doing more tasks on their own with a better understanding of the market, will demand more expertise and service quality from employees.

They expect mature interactions with a brand at each step of the journey through the pre-purchase, purchase and after-sales channels. Mature interactions mean non-standardised, reactive, direct, authentic and transparent answers from a company (see Table 37.1). They also reinforce the necessity to offer a multi-channel, seamless journey to the customer. Over-connected and over-informed customers no longer accept incoherent answers between the different points of contact.

A recent study[1] has shown the high level of expectations of over-connected customers and the risk taken by companies that do not manage them. Interestingly, it is a no-choice/no-return situation: companies have to accept and deal with new customer power.

In such an environment – and as a side-effect – the more mature the relationship with the customer, the more complex it becomes to trigger a "Wow!" effect.

Understand how to generate a "Wow!" effect through employee empowerment

The "Wow!" effect is generated by personalisation and therefore relies to a large extent on employee empowerment.

"Wow!" is emotional and subjective. Customers' perceptions will very much depend on their culture, expectations, former experiences, current situation and sector-specific usages. For example, as far as culture is concerned, brand activity

Table 37.1 New criteria for interaction with over-connected, over-informed customer (source BearingPoint)

Company behaviour in a traditional customer management interaction	Company behaviour expected by over-connected and over-informed customers
Keep high-profile: standardise answer depending on specific situation *Example:* "Depending on your problem, you will be oriented through a specific channel to specific experts"	**Be a Sherpa:** show your concern and involvement *Example:* "We may not have the answer but I personally will manage to find a solution"
React: analyse customer questions and build an answer for next time	**Anticipate:** do not wait for a customer call
Build an official answer: take time to build an official answer	**Be direct, authentic and transparent:** prefer on-the-fly reaction in a Sherpa mode
Make sure to keep control	**Make sure to keep the relationship**

on social media platforms may be considered as intrusive in Europe but as very common in China. Therefore, defining a "Wow!" programme requires a perfect and global understanding of customers and the ability to offer personalised products or services. But it is no longer enough.

To maximise the impact, "Wow!" treatments must be applied to the critical moments of the customer journey. A dramatic change is also required in the way companies measure customer management efficiency and how they manage each critical journey step whatever the channel.

Companies must shift from process and cost optimisation to personalisation and customer empowerment and then to employee empowerment.

For example, in a call centre the performance is no longer "how quick the call can be" but "how to transform the customer into a brand ambassador" (see Table 37.2). If we consider 20% of repeat calls stemmed from emotional disconnects between customers and reps, companies can easily understand the importance of customer-employee reconnection.

The idea is not to forget process optimisation, but to implement a four-step approach to employee empowerment (see Figure 37.1).

Table 37.2 Evolution of performance measurement and focus in call centres (source BearingPoint)

	What is important in call centre customer management...	Implies a focus on...	... with specific KPIs
Yesterday	Reduce ACD (Average Call Duration)	Process optimisation and industrialisation	CoS (Cost of Support) FCR (First Contact Resolution)
Today	"Once and done"	Process optimisation and industrialisation Personalised approach by customer segments Customer empowerment (self-care)	CoS (Cost of Support) FCR (First Contact Resolution) CSAT (Customer Satisfaction)
Tomorrow	Once and ...**anticipated**	**Employee empowerment**	NPS (Net Promoter Score): "Would you recommend our product or services to a friend ?"

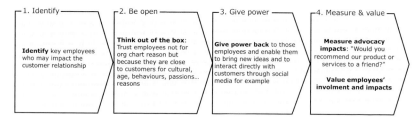

Figure 37.1 Four steps to empowering your employees (source BearingPoint)

Reduce the "employee digital divide"

The "digital divide" has been seen as an internet and mobile access issue for a long time. With more than two billion internet users in 2010, major efforts by governments and NGOs (e.g. French government policy[2] or the "Infothela" initiative in India), technology developments like cloud computing and huge investments by large operators (e.g. the $39 billion ticket paid by the American operator AT&T to buy T-Mobile in March 2011), the "digital divide" in terms of access is not over but it does seem to reduce year by year.

In fact the issue is no longer access – it has shifted to an "employee digital divide". Examples include poor equipment, zero or limited access to the internet and most often no access to social media for security or communication policies, organisational and governance constraints restricting communication with customers, and over-standardised processes limiting employee understanding of the customer journey.

If customers are said to be over-connected, over-informed, over-equipped and over-empowered, employees' connection with the outside world is often limited, they are poorly equipped ("how long does it take to start your computer, can you watch video content, do you have a smartphone?") and are partially informed, with limited autonomy to address customer issues. One of the key success factors in empowering employees is to reinvent the digital workplace and make sure they have access to collaborative solutions connected to social media (Facebook, Twitter, etc.) through up-to-date devices. But, above all, a new management approach and HR policies have to be invented.

Imagine a new management approach benefiting from employee empowerment

Empowering employees is a question of trust and courage based on a test and learn approach. Companies will have to become less controlling and more willing to trust employees. A good way to manage this process it is to understand that employees are already connected and already share knowledge and information with the outside world. So the idea should be: trust first, connect employees and customers, control after.

Companies will also have to invent specific work contracts enabling employees to answer customers anywhere, anytime through any device. The question will also be how to reward employees and to take into account KPIs like Net Promoter Score improvement. New employees are looking for new management rules based on the same kind of empowered customer expectations: autonomy, transparency and relation-oriented.

For companies that manage to empower their employees through customer relationships, the business benefits may be huge. For example:

- LoyaltyOne (operator of the Air Miles reward programme) reduced repeated contacts by 11%.

- Osram Sylvania (a lighting company) lowered its Customer Effort Score from 2.8 to 2.2, 18.5% below the average we see for B2B companies.
- Best Buy built a Twitter help-force to allow its employees to answer and resolve customer complaints via Twitter.

As we have seen, employee empowerment offers great scope to innovate and impact the "Wow!" effect for customers. Every company should explore their employee empowerment potential as a way of addressing customer and employee expectations. But there are no easy answers or "off-the-shelf" strategies. An employee empowerment approach is powerful but complex to implement. Based on their unique culture, positioning, and HR and IT policies, companies will have to face many obstacles and will need to develop specific and tailor-made methodologies if they are to secure all the benefits (see Figure 37.2).

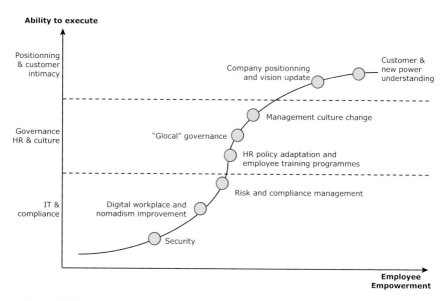

Figure 37.2 Examples of key success factors for an employee empowerment policy (source BearingPoint)

Notes

1. Bernoff J. and Schadler E. (2010) *Empowered*, Harvard Business Review Press.
2. See the BearingPoint June 2010 study, *The Digital Divide*.

Nurture and grow digital skills and competences

OPERATING IN THE DIGITAL LANDSCAPE REQUIRES THE
CLOSE COORDINATION OF MANY SPECIALIST SKILLS LIKE
MARKETING, COMMUNICATION, BUSINESS, TECHNOLOGY
AND DESIGN. DESPITE DIVERSE INTERNAL AND EXTERNAL
PROFILES, KEEPING THE ORGANISATION AGILE ENOUGH
AND ATTRACTING TALENT IS A CHALLENGE.

A shift towards digital competences to free data and services

"Digital" entered the enterprise around 15 years ago. Before the emergence of the web, information technology applications were largely deployed to manage structured data. But those applications were only available to employees within the enterprise, or at least integrated with their equivalent by third party commercial partners. Digital introduced a new era that emphasises unstructured information and free structured data from large enterprise applications (ERP, CRM and mainframe) through web services. Beyond that, a new set of devices were deployed, deriving from the personal sector and leading to new professional applications.

In order to follow the digital wave, enterprises traditionally asked their CIO (Chief Information Officer) to deploy information technology infrastructure. In parallel, marketing departments sourced external service providers to build the enterprise's web profile (e.g. the corporate website, product presentation website, online games). Established businesses have been impacted by digital – e.g. advertisers, press relationship managers, business intelligence (BI) managers – and, at the same time, new businesses have appeared, most of them with imprecise objectives, like community managers, e-business managers, web marketers, digital strategists, social media officers, webmasters and web analysts.

For all companies, the key question is: which KPI to use to evaluate these people? And an underlying question is: what are the job definitions for these businesses? In order to help HR people build a career path for the new businesses, the French Ministry of Digital Development has proposed an "overview" for such businesses (http://www.metiers.internet.gouv.fr/). This is a starter tool for HR people, helping them define the jobs needed if an enterprise is to operate in the digital world. This is the first step of a process that will have to be repeated every year in order to keep track of the evolution of such businesses.

Mobilising HR for the digital company

For an ambitious enterprise, mobilising the competences that make digital work is key: identifying required profiles, ensuring that workers use best practices (taking into account that those best practices are invented every day) and building a long-term loyalty programme for employees. In parallel, digital initiatives will have to be coordinated. Local and self-digital experiences will have to be capitalised and shared, essentially within large international companies, in order for the digital expertise to be kept within the enterprise. This mobilisation effort mixing marketing, technology and business competences, is focused on delivering business value for the enterprise and involves three main drivers: (a) new usages that customers and employees deploy every day; (b) transverse collaboration throughout the organisation; and (c) continuous innovation (see Figure 38.1).

Addressing key challenges around digital competences

Enterprises now consider digital as a business driver, involving target-based decisions taken at the highest level of organisations. Digital projects are becoming increasingly important and are attracting more and more resources. But required competences remain in short supply. General training schools do not prepare enough students, and there are no specialised institutes devoted to the digital know-how. So far, most of the schools have only set up basic knowledge training. It is essential for digital workers to have, as a minimum, a high-level understanding of marketing and technology on these issues.

Digital HR Organization drivers

Figure 38.1 The mobilisation effort (source BearingPoint)

To meet this need for specialists in Europe, three entrepreneurs in the digital sector – Xavier Niel (Free), Jacques-Antoine Granjon (Vente-privée) and Marc Simoncini (Meetic) – have joined forces to create the EEMI (Ecole européenne des métiers de l'Internet), a school dedicated to internet jobs. This kind of college is expected to help supply companies with well-trained recruits, but another factor has to be taken into account by HR departments. The existing digital workforce is highly mobile and, as the economic crisis winds down, they will be seeking more interesting jobs, on more strategic projects, within organisations that recognise their value. This mobility will impact companies as well as providers. Projects will be delayed and quality will suffer.

Preparing for the future

It is time to invest in core competences. HR departments must understand the jobs carried out within the organisation, and must identify training courses and conferences suitable for employees, ensuring that best practices are documented and shared with colleagues, organising the development of employees within the different specialised subsidiaries of the company and valuating the expertise of in-house digital experts. This last point can be achieved by encouraging the natural ability of people involved in the digital domain to share expertise with colleagues (as they do as a matter of course outside the company through social networks). For new technologies or techniques, a partnership with specialised boutiques is useful, with the enterprise carefully managing services provided by the partner.

For example, to moderate communities' websites, Orange has sourced a moderation provider. On behalf of Orange, this company moderates content generated by users. An Orange employee manages the relationship with the provider, defines the terms of the moderation charter, sets out moderation KPIs and coordinates related competences including IT, marketing, business and legal. Because this kind of expertise is considered essential for developing the business plan, it is also essential to define a career path for this employee.

Digital – even non-physical– lives thanks to men and women who build their job descriptions day-by-day as technologies and usages are evolving. Gathering such talents, and coordinating them despite obstacles, is key for the company. It is vital to begin today to understand their jobs, while giving them the freedom to evolve and adapt as digital reaches maturity.

Adapt lean philosophy to marketing

THE LEAN APPROACH TO MARKETING, INVOLVING EMPLOYEES,
PROVIDES AN EXCELLENT FRAMEWORK FOR IMPROVING THE
PERFORMANCE OF THE WHOLE COMMUNITY OF PEOPLE WHO MIGHT
NOT BE MARKETERS BUT WHO DO HAVE A STRONG INFLUENCE ON
THE CUSTOMER EXPERIENCE YOU ARE TRYING TO OPTIMISE.

The "extended marketing community"

Many experiences your customers have with your company are organised or executed by people outside your marketing department – for instance by country organisations, dealers' service staff, telephone operators, retail partners and fellow consumers, whom we can jointly call the "extended marketing community". With the development of the internet, the arrival of the empowered, informed customer and the fragmentation of attention in conventional media, the interaction of your customer with your extended marketing community is of increasing importance.

Any time spent on interactions with a customer that is not relevant to that customer or inconsistent with your intention is a waste of effort – it is a loss. How can you make sure these losses are minimised? How can you ensure that the activities in the community deliver maximum quality in the customer interaction – to improve relevance and ensure consistency?

For world-class marketing it is essential to maximise quality and minimise the losses, expanding your paradigm beyond that of creating great brands, to include focus on the behaviour and performance of your marketing community. This requires a paradigm shift from a check and control culture that focused on traditional marketing creation to a learning organisation that is continuously optimising the customer experience.

Lean is an excellent framework with which to turn such a large, dispersed marketing community around, freeing up resources by reducing losses, implementing a strong measurement framework, shifting the focus to building capabilities in the community and organising empowered teams close to the customer.

Align the objectives of your community

Underpinning a lean marketing programme should be an accepted definition of waste or losses. If you have invested heavily in creating a customer and have enticed them to visit your store, you want to be sure that the experience in that store is consistent with what was promised. Otherwise you might lose the investment or, even worse, the customer.

The loss structure forms a central spine in ensuring the programme delivers tangible results that you are looking for. To make sure your marketing community acts to reduce losses, in line with the plan, the members of your community need to understand your intentions, your product, your brand, the profile of the customers you are after and the value of getting their contribution right.

Many members of your community will not be as aware of your brand or intentions as you are. Their exposure to your ideas might be limited to just your advertising. You start to engage your community by building up communication processes that distribute a consistent message on the product, the brand, and the performance for each introduction and each campaign. This communication should transfer all the information necessary to make for good decisions at customer contact.

For example, by simply making information available to sales reps in a multi-brand store, you might make it easier for them to engage with a customer on your product and create a strong positive bias. This might include some questions that support an on-the-spot segmentation of the customer.

Improve understanding at customer touch point

The interaction with your customer is a cyclical process. The shorter the loop of the cycle, the more engaged your customer, the greater the impact of your activities. The shortest and tightest loop is direct conversation with someone in your community. This is where you can make a difference much more effectively than via mass media like broadcasting a commercial. This is also the most expensive customer contact – one-to-one interaction. At this critical, cost-intensive moment you want to make sure that the interaction is consistent and relevant. The only way to achieve this is by building up the skills and capabilities of community members handling the contact.

With lean, we focus on the activities where employees can make the most difference. All other activities are standardised where possible. Lean enables people by involving them in improvement projects (*Kaizen*), thus building up an understanding of how their action impacts the customer improvements you want to achieve.

This is also where the loss structure is operationalised. If the primary process of the people at the point of contact is enhancing the customer experience through relevant and consistent dialogue, the focus should be on how to improve the interaction in order to improve the customer experience in order to improve the value of those customers in sales terms.

Improvement projects can start from a quite simple premise, such as how to make sure that the right sales materials are available at the point of sale. Straightforward projects like this result in instant improvements to working conditions, they generate support and train people in the process. At the same time, they form a foundation for achieving greater control of your customer interaction activities.

Empower the community to accelerate results

Lean programmes typically start with a pilot that proofs the principle and builds support on a small scale. Successful pilots allow you to make a start on the programme, and gain insight and build traction. The focus allows you to ensure that sufficient resources are available to ensure success.

In marketing, the best focus for a pilot is a campaign or product introduction. This is much more effective than focusing on a geographic area. The inherent interest and attention that is generated by an exciting campaign or product introduction facilitates the establishment of key metrics and supports the engagement required. With engagement initiated and understanding of the process growing, you start to fuel the programme by allocating responsibilities and resources. A guiding principle for executing such a programme is to balance empowerment and availability of means with level of understanding and clarity of focus. A typical example is to give service staff the authority to settle complaints within a budget. There are many other examples such as delegating campaign and media mix selection to the outlet manager so that it can be fine-tuned to the local situation.

In the process of implementing a lean programme, some basic systems and structures in the company might be affected that could threaten the success of your programme, so you need to enlist the support of the people at the top to help address any issues arising. Usually, if the top is supportive, the bottom of the pyramid is supportive. Most resistance will come from the middle layers. Their position is often based on experience, which might become obsolete once the organisation starts learning at the point of contact.

In the marketing community the top and the middle layers are not so clear because, rather than a hierarchical organisation, it is a collection of people from your department, other departments, suppliers, trade relations and retail partners. This is helpful in the sense that you have full control over the content and the knowledge, but it might be a hindrance in the sense that you can't directly make resources and time available for the people involved. You will need to invest resources in the programme to entice these people to work with you. Given the importance of the customer experience in the marketing arena, this money might just be the right investment to gain maximum return.

Use lean to empower your customer touch points

FROM CUSTOMISED CARS TO CUSTOMISED CAMPAIGNS...

In 1909 Henry Ford said, "Any customer can have a car painted any colour that he wants so long as it is black". Imagine the amazement of the Toyota factory manager 40 years later when he was asked to produce a different car for each customer. Today, it must feel just as awkward for the marketing manager if you asked them to develop campaigns for individual customers. Just as car factories around the world tackled this transformation using lean, marketing departments should use lean if they want to open up their marketing organisation to customer dialogue.

So why would companies want to focus on customer dialogue and move away from pushing mass campaigns to customers? Customer experience has become the next competitive battleground and many organisations miss out on revenue because they are unable to efficiently deliver consistent and relevant messages across all channels, products and functions to their prospects and customers. The traditional "product push" outbound campaigning approaches don't reach a large part of their client base, thereby missing the opportunity to create a good customer experience.

"Dialogue management" is a multi-channel "pull" concept that aims to establish customer interaction in a continuous flow. The campaign is no longer the driver for marketing actions, the dialogue is. Dialogues should be thoughtfully designed based on customer insights (often already available) and commercial objectives. By first targeting and understanding customers, companies can define the desired customer experience. Optimising customer analytics is crucial here; move from standard reports that tell what has happened to predictive modelling and optimisation; what's the best that can happen? With that information, companies can start designing dialogue programmes. This is the foundation of future marketing: dialogue management.

Lean is a key capability, shifting companies from monologue to dialogue

How can an organisation manage this shift towards customised campaigns and customer interaction? Especially now that channel complexity is increasing, customer expectations are high and marketing funds are limited. Having such a customer-centric marketing organisation will result in a dramatic increase in the number of campaigns and interactions with the customer. Just imagine that these huge number of campaigns need to be organised following the current marketing processes and structure: lead times, approval cycles, piles of work in progress on people's desks, re-work, last minute changes and no control over contact frequency. How to decide which campaign to use, for which customer using what channel/interaction? Even worse, these decisions have to be made in a split second because dialogues are often triggered by the customer, which requires real-time dialogue management.

This challenge cannot be met just by implementation of the right tool – it is about supporting organisation-wide profitable growth by applying the right set of techniques supported by superior processes, organisation and technology.

To be able to move from push to pull campaigns, the organisation needs to be shaped for dialogue. A customer-centric treatment across channels and products requires integration of organisational silos, resulting in more efficiency and quality through less inconsistencies. Furthermore, advanced campaign techniques need to be applied and the campaign management processes and IT should be industrialised. This results in improved efficiency of the marketing organisation leading to lower costs, reduced time to market and shorter cycle times. Inefficiencies due to non-value-adding activities, inflexibility and weak customer experience are avoided.

In most cases there is enough room for improvement. In fact, more than 80% of activities in current typical marketing operations processes do not add any value.

Process redesign to reduce waste and increase flexibility

First focus in a lean marketing programme should be on process analysis. How processes are described is very different from how they are executed: reality is often more complex due to wasteful activities (see Figure 40.1).

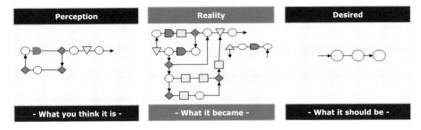

Figure 40.1 Complex reality (source BearingPoint)

Focus on reducing non-value-added activities. Typical forms of waste in the marketing process include approvals, re-work, information seeking and sharing. Re-engineering the process to allow customer dialogue by changing the way things are done, with lean principles in mind. Specialise and centralise where possible, and remove sequentials and steps where possible. Shift tasks and roles and responsibilities when more efficient, and organise pre-authorisation early in the process by defining the right governance and delegation of responsibilities.

Reducing lead time dramatically means less campaigns are under construction at any one moment, further simplifying your operation. Standardising work methods for developing campaigns can further dramatically increase productivity. There will be more time for value-adding activities such as customer insight, value proposition development, creative process and execution.

By examining the issues in the processes, the root causes are determined. Root cause analysis gives insights into how waste is created and how bottlenecks can be removed, thus making the process lean.

When redesigning processes they need to become flexible so as to tailor offers to match customer needs at the point of interaction. After removing waste, dialogues should be made possible by making decision rules central to the marketing system.

Lean is all about organising processes towards realising clearly set goals. Therefore sustainable improvement is only possible if work is done with a control mechanism that measures success and integrates feedback. This will increase marketing accountability for results and foster continuous improvement at a strategic, tactical and operational level. Examples of such metrics are return on marketing investments (ROMI) and time to market.

Manage by example

Lean has shown that this is feasible if the organisation as a whole is involved. Continuous improvement and reduction of waste will need to be part of not only the marketing department's brief, but also that of everyone else involved in the customer journey.

Managing this change requires more than shuffling some chairs on the deck of the Titanic... optimisation of the current situation is not enough. This means that any successful lean programme needs to be supported or even managed by the top. Management should be visible during the improvement process and should lead by example. There should be a willingness to change the way work flows through an entire organisation, not just one department. The improvements should be based on a dialogue with the employees involved – a dialogue that will form a good example for the kind of dialogue to start with customers.

Measure your digital effectiveness

Is "digital" worth investing in? That is no longer the point. Digital activities do bring value to companies – increased turnover, enhanced loyalty, improved satisfaction, reduced costs, etc. Key questions are: What is digital ROI? To what extent does digital enable companies to achieve their goals? Which key performance indicators are relevant for digital? Who in the company is interested in which indicators? What tools are required?

"Digital" contributes to overall company goals in three ways: the revenues that it generates (additional turnover, new customers); the relationship that it creates and the experience with the brand that it allows through the intensity of communication; and the proximity enabled by new usages. Digital initiatives and projects are mostly based on innovative technologies; however, the right KPIs do not have to be innovative. To control KPI efficiency, organisations need the right tools and skills (see Figure 41.1).

Secure digital enablers

Digital enablers form the base of the pyramid. Without them, nothing (or almost nothing) is possible. Indicators cover the loading time of a web page, e-commerce turnover, number of loads of an application or of a video, organisational layers or

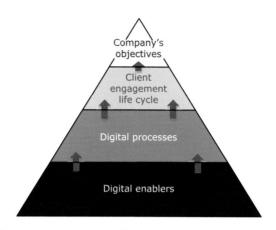

Figure 41.1 Measuring effectiveness (source BearingPoint)

presence in geographical zones, buying-path steps, drop-out rate, preferred shipping modes, etc.

Measure the performance of digital processes

Digital processes are the heart of digital. *Transactions* are based on sales funnel, leads management, cross-selling, promotion and marketing campaign – whether from a catalogue, a video or a buying-path. *Relational* processes rely on blogs, communities, social networks and e-reputation management. *Experience* can be enriched by augmented reality. These three types of digital processes (transact, relate, experience) require indicators: click-through, response rate, lead generation, average time per session, cross-selling efficiency, net promoter score, number of visits before a purchase or word of mouth (e.g. buzz generated in social networks, blogs, instant messages). In 2010, Kraft Foods' Oreo, number three brand page on Facebook, had a fan base of over 10.1 million, growing at a rate of 71,000 new fans each a day.[1] At the same time their official website, NabiscoWorld.com, had seen US traffic drop from 1.2 million in July 2009 to just 321,000 a year later.[2] Such KPIs are essential in monitoring digital activities and guiding digital choices.

Value digital impact on customer life cycle

While measuring efficiency of processes, eventually the objective is to enhance clients' commitment to the brand. Leaders in customer experience – Amazon, Apple, Tesco and Wal-Mart – are taking a comprehensive approach in order to understand the impact of customer experience management across client life cycle. This enables focus on the products/services that provide the highest return. Client life cycle indicators that can be measured are brand awareness or reputation, requests for information, engagement with web content and increased knowledge of customers. A survey by the Online Publishers Association shows that consumers exposed to display advertising spent over 50% more time than the average visitor to these sites the next month.[3] These significant lifts would be overlooked (see Figure 41.2) if one only considered immediate actions (e.g. click-through rates).

Figure 41.2 Define metrics across customer life cycle (source BearingPoint)

Indicators used to measure transactions, relationships and experience performance are available at all levels (enablers, processes or life cycle management) and can be cross levels. The aggregation of these indicators with non-digital indicators gives the opportunity to measure the contribution of digital to the company's objectives.

Adapt KPI to the audience

In major groups with an Executive Committee made of +50-year-old-members, unlike controlling KPIs, which have been known for years, a specific effort on clarity and pedagogy is required to communicate on digital metrics.

To meet C-level expectations, digital should be closely linked to either revenues or brand image. As with any other departments, digital indicators should be limited to simplify and reinforce messages; hence the importance of their choice. C-level indicators do not have to be innovative (see Figure 41.3); they should be *Aggregate digital and non-digital indicators* strongly linked to existing ones (contribution to sales, reputation impact, etc.). Digital KPIs are essential for digital projects communication throughout the company, from service quality analysis, relevant to the IS department, to global digital performance, key for C-level management.

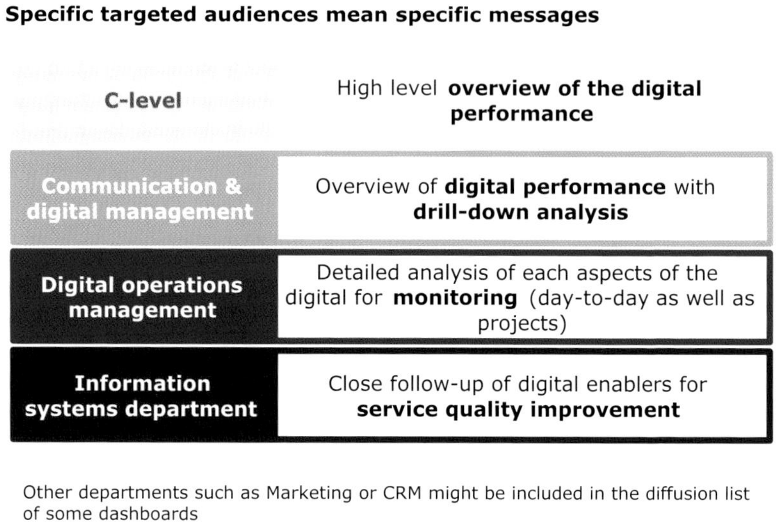

Specific targeted audiences mean specific messages

C-level	High level **overview of the digital performance**
Communication & digital management	Overview of **digital performance** with **drill-down analysis**
Digital operations management	Detailed analysis of each aspects of the digital for **monitoring** (day-to-day as well as projects)
Information systems department	Close follow-up of digital enablers for **service quality improvement**

Other departments such as Marketing or CRM might be included in the diffusion list of some dashboards

Figure 41.3 Adapting to the audience

Client as the direct user

What has digital changed? The client is often the direct user (website, applications), so service levels expected and actually provided have to be followed up closely. Whatever the functionalities provided, response time or security cannot be disregarded. Indicators must trigger what is efficient and what can be optimised. An indicator should indeed be actionable – i.e. company operations can impact on the indicator value. Traditional indicators such as advertisement audience choice and Gross Rating Point measures have to take new axes into consideration. Digital initiatives require operational indicators to measure their success or failure and, again, to identify potential optimisations: e.g. reach, time spent on a sales tunnel path and drop-out rate at each step. If time spent filling in forms is a cause for not going through the process, the company can look for alternative ways such as open ID across companies. Thus, on Chronopost or Deezer, customers can log in using their Orange mobile phone number as ID. French government agencies and some private sector companies (e.g. utilities) have created a unique portal to update an address and organise a house move.

Over and above language and cultural factors, digital reach raises wider issues than most traditional communication means like stores or magazines. For example, as bandwidth is very low in China, companies targeting this emerging market will have to provide specific solutions – e.g. to create content for a light website and to favour mobile internet, as its ramping is faster than desktop internet. The KPI axes will have to adapt too: while focusing relationship activities on Facebook in English-speaking countries makes sense, metrics should be reviewed in Asia to consider other networks. Indeed, Facebook is still far behind Mixi, Gree and Mobage-town. Each has more than 20 million users, while Facebook has only 2 million users in Japan.[4]

Digital KPIs require BI to adapt

What is to be measured has changed. Digital technologies give the opportunity to collect new types of data in many different ways. Most relevant indicators already exist in the bricks and mortar world: e.g. transformation ratios, traffic ratios, Gross Rating Point, revenues, cost per contact, Once and done ratio or additional sales. However, the way to collect the source data, to analyse it and follow-up actions will differ.

Business intelligence (BI) tools have to take these new factors into account. While designing a website, or an application, legacy systems should be considered. Data will have to be exchangeable and compared. New data and new axes will have to be integrated in the existing systems (customer database, dataware-house, dashboards) to secure analysis quality and to enable comparison with bricks and mortar. One of the keys, and frequently an issue, will be to identify a customer across the company. As a first step, this can be done by a manual survey or a statement in shops; it can then be automated and further enriched with the creation and use of a unique identifier. A customer account should be defined thinking of custom-ers' expectations outside the digital world. At the same time, KPIs will rely on new tools such as tagging plan and survey, and should favour behavioural analysis when the customer is not identified instead of requiring a systematic identification.

What is to be measured has changed

BI organisation will have to adapt. Make sure you build it with the right competences. To get digital expertise, before recruiting, call in partners; create relations with digital agencies and editors. Once initiatives are valued within the company you can recruit expert people who will be attracted by your activities and the challenges ahead. The Digital Team will have to work closely with marketing, CRM and the IS department to create a common indicators reference.

Notes

1. In February 2011 the Oreo fan base reached 16.8 million and had won a Guinness record for the number of new fans in 24 hours.
2. Source AdAge.com, 23 August 2010: "What Happens When Facebook Trumps Your Brand Site?"
3. Source *The Silent Click: Building Brands Online*, conducted by the Online Publishers Association in partnership with comScore, June 2009.
4. Source *The New York Times*, 9 January 2011, "Facebook Wins Relatively Few Friends in Japan".

Implement new
Key Performance Indicators

MANY KPIS CAN BE DEFINED TO MEASURE THE SUCCESS OF
SERVICE DEPARTMENTS. MANAGERS NEED TO BE EQUIPPED WITH
A STRUCTURED AND PRAGMATIC FRAMEWORK THAT HELPS THEM
SELECT THE "RIGHT" KPIS TO BETTER STEER THEIR BUSINESS.

Expectations for customer service organisations today are high, expressed in increased efficiency – i.e. providing the same or even improved service levels at constant or lower costs. But with higher investment in the new digital channels has come dramatically greater complexity, which has to be managed.

So close interaction of optimised processes is required, an efficient organisational set-up and appropriate IT infrastructure. A prerequisite for measuring success is a sufficient information base – i.e. the key performance indicators (KPIs) of customer service need be defined and established. Typically we meet two very different kinds of problems: either many KPIs are defined in a deficient way or not available at all; or (more frequently) there is an information overflow and it is unclear which of the KPIs are the most significant.

A balanced scorecard for service

There are literarily dozens of possible value drivers and strategic measures for customer service. Our approach to choosing the most suitable measures is based on the balanced scorecard (BSC) model. Similar to the classical BSC, our model is based on four dimensions that define and control the steering parameters (see Figure 42.1).

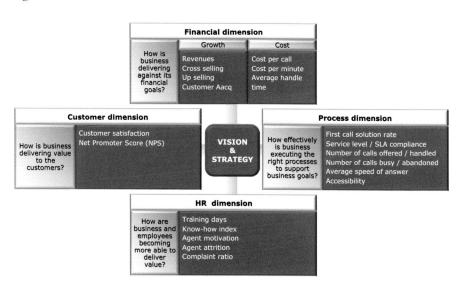

Figure 42.1 Four-dimensional BSC model (source BearingPoint)

Financial dimension

Within classical service organisations with no sales, only cost parameters are part of the BSC. The most important KPIs are the usual ones: cost per call, cost per minute for call centres, or cost per case for service centres. Today we are in a transition to "hybrid" structures, with sales targets increasingly important at many service units. Here it will be mandatory to enhance financial KPIs with additional revenue KPIs (see below).

Process dimension

Operational-level KPIs include on the one hand those that directly influence financial goals (e.g. cycle time per case, average talk time per call, etc.), while on the other hand there are parameters relating to process quality, like FCS (First

Call Solution Rate) or repeater complaints (i.e. complaints on the customer service process). Here we also find classical call centre KPIs like Accessibility and Service Level Compliance.

HR dimension

The external impact of service organisations is not determined by process quality alone, but very directly by the capabilities of employees. While FCS remains a strong indicator on the process side, on the HR side this can be tracked by the number of training sessions conducted and the number of training days. The possibility of enlisting support from the team manager/supervisor could be a good indicator here, in which case the management-to-staff ratio is the correct indicator (which today normally falls within a broad range of between 1 to 5 and 1 to 40). All these dimensions have an impact on the external perspective of the customer.

Customer dimension

We (rightly) assume a positive correlation between service centre quality KPIs, like Accessibility, and customer satisfaction. A regular check on this relationship is essential, via surveys or pointed questions at the end of each service case.

Next we examine the two big changes currently affecting modern service organisations and having a significant impact on our model – the increasing importance of inbound sales and social media.

Change no. 1: The growing importance of inbound sales

The idea that each customer contact should be used as a sales contact is not particularly new, but obstacles, especially legal restrictions for outbound call centres, have forced companies to develop new ideas for selling their products. Why not use the people with the highest-end customer contact rate – i.e. customer service employees? There are several possibilities: the direct way uses the service call itself to promote, explain and eventually sell new products; the indirect way adds an extra step, with information gathered during the service call being forwarded to colleagues in the sales department. This intermediate step is particularly necessary with major complaints, where the direct approach to inbound sales has a very negative effect on client satisfaction. Nevertheless, and despite the sensitivity of the whole topic, a growing number of companies regard inbound sales as the major growth channel of the future.

Change no. 2: Customer service and social media

Everybody is talking about social media and the possible impact on business operational models. Currently, most activities in this area are driven by the marketing department, but arguably the most significant impact here will focus on customer service, as regular customer service processes are taken over by social media communities. Many companies in the high-tech sector are leading the way here (some of them by accident), as a major share of service requests (even, and sometimes especially, the more complex ones) are handled by the members of online communities. Estimates suggest that such outsourcing could lead to cost savings of around 40%.[1]

Implications for the KPI scorecard

Both these trends are having a major impact on the operating model of companies and their service units. Management has to ensure these trends are taken into account within the BSC framework. For inbound sales this task is quite easy: in general, the same KPIs can be used that are already part of the sales department's KPI framework. In addition, sales success should be correlated with the volume of emerging service requests (e.g. "#Inbound leads" / "#Service requests" or, even stronger, "#Inbound orders" / "#Service requests".

The quantitative measurement of social media activities is much harder to achieve. This is because, by definition, they take place outside the company, and therefore the assessment and evaluation of the data is a much more difficult task. Nevertheless, it is important to measure the volume of service requests (SRs) handled "outside". A suitable KPI could be the ratio #SR internal / #SR external.[2] Another important parameter is the efficiency of the community itself. A typical web community has a ratio of 1 / 9 / 90 of "key opinion leaders" to "contributors" to "readers only". Companies should aim to change this indicator in favour of higher numbers of contributors and key players. Companies have already recognised the huge importance of key opinion leaders in these forums and are trying to develop suitable means to increase their number and to influence their behaviour in a positive way.[3] First studies indicate that the ratio can be developed towards 1 / 5 / 40.

Overall, the total number of performance indicators should not exceed 15 (including new inbound sales and social media KPIs). In consequence, customer service managers need to shed lower priority KPIs to avoid exceeding this total. That is the only way to avoid the information overflow described at the start of this chapter. In our experience, the occasional removal of KPIs is as necessary (and just as difficult) as the creation of new ones.

Notes

1. See also Gartner (2010) "Top Use Cases and Benefits for Successful Social CRM", December.
2. For the "external" SR volume, rough estimations will be the first step – e.g. the assessment of the "Top 5" communities and extrapolation of their volume.
3. Because key opinion leaders are extremely sensitive about the possibility of their being manipulated, these actions have to be defined very carefully.

Conclusions

Navigating the digital paradoxes

MOST BUSINESS BOOKS TRY TO GIVE ANSWERS. THEY TYPICALLY START WITH A DESCRIPTION OF THE BUSINESS LANDSCAPE AND THEN LAY OUT A RECIPE FOR WHAT YOU SHOULD DO TO COMPETE AND WIN. THE FACT THAT WE HAVE INSTEAD PRESENTED AND DISCUSSED A SET OF PARADOXES IS RECOGNITION THAT THERE ARE STILL TOO MANY UNANSWERED QUESTIONS FOR ANYONE TO OFFER A "ONE SIZE FITS ALL" SOLUTION.

As shown in the Figure C.1, across the five paradoxes (Chapters 1-5) there are several recurring themes. Underlying all these themes is the importance of recognising that the paradoxes relate to companies innovating in relation to new modes of economic interaction and new modes of digital interaction, as shown in Figure C.2.

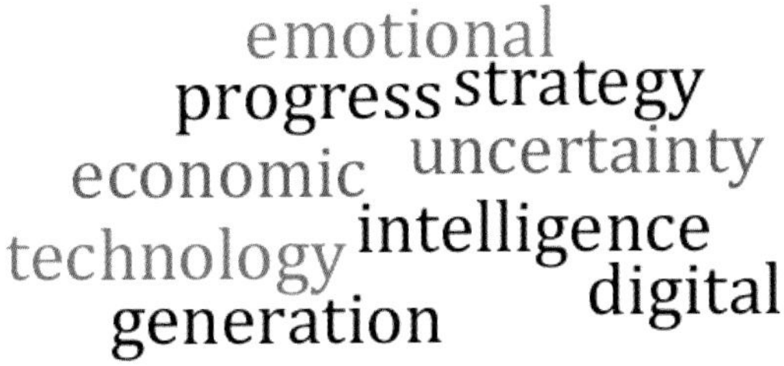

emotional
progress strategy
economic uncertainty
technology intelligence
generation digital

Figure C.1 Paradox themes

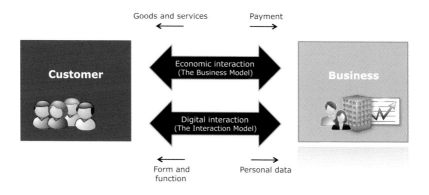

Figure C.2 Economic and digital interactions

Generational differences characterise openness to engaging with digital

The first theme is that there are big differences between the generations in their attitudes to digital technologies and the issues these technologies raise. The 10-15 years of the internet is a short time compared with people's lifetimes. It is not surprising that it matters whereabouts in a person's life that the revolution has occurred; psychological flexibility matters and changes over lifetime.

Innovations in economic models and the deployment of digital technologies need to be managed together for success, and different segments offer different opportunities for exploitation (see Figure C.3).

For each of the paradoxes it is easy to identify which pole is associated with the digital generation and which pole is associated with the toe-dippers. The applications typically used by these groups also differ, as illustrated in Figure C.4.

The digital generation has been the most comfortable with digital technologies, historically being the early adopters and therefore the engine of progress. But this generation does not have the buying power that it did. The under-25s are particularly hard hit by the current recession, with unemployment rates edging towards 50% among this age group in even quite developed economies such as Spain. Many companies are going to have to adapt their digital strategies to appeal to a wider span of consumers.

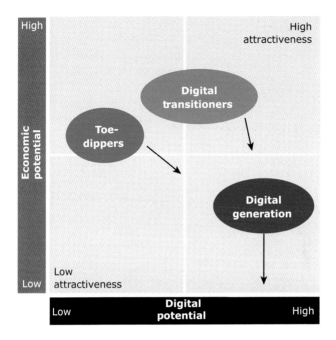

Figure C.3 Economic and digital potential

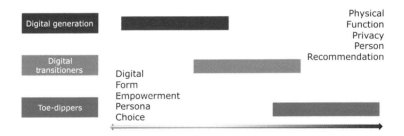

Figure C.4 Applications used by generational segments

Strategies must take account of uncertainty over the direction of new technical innovations

The second major theme is the uncertainty over how technology will progress. As we saw in Chapter 1 (Paradox 1), the interplay between the physical world and the digital world is not linear. Initially, digital products and services substituted for physical ones; then came ways of integrating physical and digital experiences; and most recently, techniques of augmented reality. The challenge is that customers value both the physical and the digital; they are not always convinced by "progress". Furthermore, not all customers think identically. An exciting experience for one customer can be an alienating experience for another.

The scale of research in internet and mobile technologies almost guarantees progress – even in traditionally daunting fields such as natural language processing. Companies cannot help but take decisions on which technologies to use, and how these technologies are configured. Often there will be little objective data on which to make decisions because technologies need to become "absorbed" into culture before they are appreciated. For example, "Facebook Questions" originated as people began using Facebook in a new and unexpected way.[1] In other words, the originators of a technology never know exactly what will be done with it. Even where no new technology is involved, there can be mistakes. The UK food store Waitrose revamped its website claiming it would be "easier and quicker". A fortnight later, and following criticism on its own online forum, the company had to admit to problems with its new website and apologise for the inconvenience and frustration caused.

Innovations in the economics of the internet have a significant role to play in defining the future

The third theme is that of the economics of the internet – of the roles of advertising, promotion and consumer targeting. The basic business model of "free" applications relies on companies being able to harvest value from personal data gathered incidentally as part of the user interaction process. As recent controversy over Facebook illustrates, there is disquiet over the loss of privacy involved.

While the first quarter of 2011 data shows that 1 in every 4 advertising euros is spent online shows that advertisers value online's ability to target customers, part of the difficulty is that "targeting" is not necessarily as highly valued by consumers. While advertisers may promise that consumers will receive only the advertising that is strictly relevant, consumers have grown used to filtering out the adverts they are not interested in, and are yet to be persuaded that their interests are at heart. The existence of telecoms bundles including broadband, TV and phone opens up the ability for consumer preferences in one medium to be applied to advertising in another. Until there is more evidence of informed consent, companies must handle the more subtle consumer targeting very carefully.

Companies acting with Emotional Intelligence will succeed better in navigating the digital future

The fourth theme is emotional intelligence (EI). To navigate the paradoxes companies need to ensure that their behaviour is appropriate to the mindsets and sensitivities of target customers for the type of product or service they provide. Of course, all behaviour should also be compliant with governing legislation.

What this means is that companies need to understand their target customers' mindset and sensitivities with sufficient acuity to enable decisions on where to position themselves in relation to location tracking, cookies and data harvesting, and the mining of customers' social networks (who they are friends with/connected to). Of course, this is easier said than done. So, how to avoid mistakes? Think of the real-world equivalent and likely consequences of behaving inappropriately – breaking trust, or being over- or under-familiar. As a simple test, check that your digital customer management approaches do not violate any established norms. So what about with regard to emerging and developing norms? Watch, and learn from others' mistakes, and successes. And experiment for yourself, but, just in case, have a clear strategy and action plan in place to manage getting it wrong.

Paradoxes are, by definition, tricky to reconcile. But in relation to customer management the digital paradoxes discussed here are ones that all companies in the modern day have a real incentive towards addressing – hitting the right balance, and behaving appropriately. Not only can you become a company providing great products and services that are genuinely valued by your end-users; by behaving appropriately you will become a trusted partner and a guardian of privacy. In other words, your customers' friend.

Note

1. http://blog.facebook.com/blog.php?post=10150110059982131

About BearingPoint

We deliver Business Consulting with Management and Technology capabilities. We are an independent firm with European roots and a global reach.

In today's world, we think that Expertise is not enough. Driven by a strong entrepreneurial mindset and desire to create long term partnerships, our 3 200 consultants are committed to creating greater client value, from strategy through to implementation, delivering tangible results.

As our clients' trusted advisor for many years (60% of Eurostoxx 50 and major public organisations), we define where to go and how to get there…

To get there. Together.

For more information: **www.bearingpointconsulting.com**

Contributors

Publication directors: Erik Campanini, Eric Falque, Sarah-Jayne Williams.

Chief editor: Michaël Tartar.

We are particularly grateful to all those who have brought this work from project to reality. Special thanks go to:

Johanna Ambil, Doug Armstrong, Nathalie Asheuer, Xavier Baudouin, Patrice Bégoc, Catherine Boidin, Pierre Brun, Erik Campanini, Maxime Canler, Férid Chakroun, Mickael Chaniot, Stéphane Chauveau, Sayah Chennoufi, Jean-Philippe Cluset, Isabelle Denervaud, Cyprien Dourster, Bruno Dreyfus, Clément Dufresne, Martine Dupuichaud, Marion Durante, Damien Ferrand, Sabrina Ferro, Kevin Fournier, Markus Franke, Jonathan Freeman, Frédéric Gigant, Carole Giraud, Martin Griffiths, Martin Hermsen, Augustin Hertz, Daniel Houser, Jean-Michel Huet, Kyle Hutchins, Marielle Jubert, Jeremy Klein, Jan Jacob Koomen, Thierry Lalande, Tanguy de La Peschardière, Jean-François Lasnier, Muriel Legendre, Alexandre Malric, Marie de Massol, Mikaël Meyer, Raphaël Monnot, Peter Mueller, Charlotte Pats, Virginie Pez, Corinne Raguenaud, Maxence Regnier, James Rodger, Folkert Ruiter, Julie Savary, Céline Schwartz, David Solal, Etienne Soumoy, Susanna Tam, Michaël Tartar, Sandra Thévenin, Guillaume Tollet, Angélique Tourneux, Judith Valstar, John Vance, Vincent Vaudour, Renaud Véron, Sarah-Jayne Williams.

The authors would also like to thank those who actively supported this project, in particular:

Olivier Chatin, Per Jacobson, Natalia Krasnoperova, Peter Mockler, Marcel Nickler, Dolf Smeets, Stefan Spohr, Hans-Werner Wurzel.